ON SACRED GROUND

Death, Trauma, and Transformation:

Memoir of an Officer Involved Shooting

Scott L. Haslar

ISBN: 978-1-66784-162-5 (Softcover)
ISBN: 978-1-66784-163-2 (eBook)

To:

All police officers passed who made the ultimate
sacrifice defending the Thin Blue Line.

All police officers present and future who will
courageously continue to defend the Thin Blue Line.

Contents

"To know peace is the way of the warrior."[1]

—Erwin Raphael McManus

DISCLAIMER

This book is a memoir that chronicles the author's experiences while employed as a law enforcement officer on the Indianapolis Metropolitan Police Department. This book is an account based on memory combined with newspaper articles covering certain events. Memory is not an exact science; however, I have tried to recreate the events with as much accuracy as possible. Names of some of the people involved have been changed to protect their privacy. All the characters you will read about are based on real people. Dialogue was based on memory, interviews with those involved, and information documented in newspaper accounts and journal entries. In some instances, time periods have been compressed in service of the narrative. When my thoughts are in italics, they are my opinion only. Thank you for allowing me to share my story with you.

Prologue

It's January 2021, the days leading up to President-elect Biden's inauguration. The new year ushered in with very little of the usual celebratory fanfare. Instead of nationwide partying, the country seemed to sit quietly at home or at socially distanced gatherings, cautiously optimistic that 2021 would offer some relief.

Surely, this year will be better than the last, I thought and hoped.

Just a few days ago, I sat in utter disbelief, glued to images of yet more violence as rioters stormed the Capitol building. Meanwhile, President Biden is pledging to reunite our polarized country. And from where I sit, in the center of the two poles, I can't imagine where he would even begin.

A recent Forbes article listed best practices for accomplishing this monumental task. A few of the suggestions are to listen to what all sides have to say, demonstrate empathy, don't cast blame, tell the truth, and find common ground—a "to do" list that sounds daunting and nearly impossible to check off in our discordant social climate.

Less than a year ago, our country was in varying degrees of COVID-19 lockdown as I was finishing the first draft of this book, which is about my involvement in a controversial officer-involved shooting that occurred in 1990. I thought 30 years' time was more than enough emotional and psychological distance to safely break my silence and offer my account of the event. I was both eager and apprehensive for some of my associates not involved in the writing process to read it and offer feedback before I sent it to an interested publisher. The very week I was readying the manuscript for the mail, George Floyd was killed.

Initially, there was common bipartisan disgust and condemnation of the event, but this unity was short-lived, because it wasn't conducive to emotionally charged platforms. I watched as the political and racial divide grew exponentially. The already-fragile fabric of police/community partnerships began to fray, and then unravel.

As I take all this in, with 30 years of hindsight, it frustrates me to see, we have not evolved. We've devolved.

My view from the center was a puzzling sight. I am quite aware this country is wrought by and steeped in violence. No one knows this better than police and military personnel. But does our history of violence justify furthering those practices to achieve balance and inclusion? Was no one else seeing this oxymoron?

In my mind, the images of man's inhumanity to man, captured and projected daily in the mainstream media, only served to reinforce the violence narrative, so much so, it is now accepted and culturally normalized within subjective good versus evil narratives—if you're not with us, you're against us. Thus, some acts of violence within protests were condoned, while others were condemned. Some politicians were lauded for encouraging raucous civil demonstrations, while others were villainized—it only depended on which side was doing the evaluating and which agenda was in pursuit.

As a retired police officer, I would assert that the majority of those in the profession, myself included, have pointed their efforts at trying to bridge the racial divides in our communities through the establishment of police/citizen partnerships. There are always exceptions, but the overarching goal in most departments is to find or build common ground. I stand firm on that.

Now that goal looks hopelessly unattainable.

The message we're hearing today is that we were the bad guys all along—the ones to be feared. We've heard the chants from protesters as their cities burned around them: "All cops are bastards." "The only good cop is a dead cop." "Pigs in a blanket, fry 'em like bacon." One protester's sign read, "Prosecute KKK Killer Cops." Some media outlets furthered a narrative suggesting the policing profession is inundated with white supremacists wearing badges. Defund the police became the left's mantra.

Just days before the inauguration, I read a friend's post who sits on the far left, whose sentiment was beginning to echo others: "Stop saying we're a divided country. It gives equal weight to both sides. We are a country with a white male supremacy problem. We don't need to find common ground. We need one side to accept the basic humanity of everyone who doesn't look like them." So much for unifying the country.

With all of this in mind, I couldn't fathom how friends who read my first draft could have all asked a similar question—where did my darkness come from? "I would like to hear more about how you found yourself in such despair," they said. How did I end up a jaded, caustic retired police officer whose baseline negative mental state starts with one foot in the grave? I was surprised that the retelling of death, destruction, and addiction that surrounded me throughout my career was not enough to illustrate how I "went dark," so to speak.

I took a walk on the beach, as close to a "happy place" as someone like me can claim. As I walked, racing thoughts led me to that subconscious stored and dormant reel of images, feelings, sensations, and scripts of 28 years spent in law enforcement. Almost immediately, the reconstitution of memories and emotions that forever anchor me to my profession—profound grief and suffering—materialized all over again, all pointing to the darkness I write about here.

I remembered pursuing a fleeing vehicle tearing down a city street. Up ahead, the car struck a woman driving home from work as she exited the highway. The impact was enough to spin her vehicle with such force, the engine block flew clean away. As I approached the woman, we exchanged a mutual silent moment of shock that she was still alive. The two suspects were ejected and lay lifeless amongst the wreckage. That stench of smoke, coolant, and fresh death is indelibly recorded in my memory.

I remembered the scene of an accident of a car that was burning. The officer who arrived first said the driver was screaming, "Help me!" as flames engulfed his body, but he couldn't save him. It was too late. After the fire was extinguished, I saw the driver's hands were still reaching out of his window, frozen in outstretched desperation and burned to a crisp. His face was scorched and blackened, resembling that of an overdone hunk of meat. It's still hard to grill in my backyard without that image invading.

I remembered watching a young boy shot and killed by another while he was playing basketball. I didn't make it to the court fast enough to intercede. By the time I got to him, his body was bleeding out, the gunman nowhere in sight.

I remembered the many suicide scenes. One in particular, I walked into a living room where the walls were still dripping with blood and pieces of brain as the ceiling fan continued to circle and spray gray matter, a shotgun his weapon of choice.

All these victims were citizens I tried to serve and protect but couldn't. And this doesn't take into account the times I used force and hurt others, ironically, in order to serve and protect.

Other officers have similar yet individual paths to that same dark destination. This particular memoir focuses on the impact of one particular incident.

Some suggested I just grow a set and get over it—stop using one exceptional event as an excuse for addiction and irresponsibility. In the policing profession, however, the up-close and personal exposure to man's inhumanity to his fellows is not an isolated experience. It's an endless stream of atrocities. As you are trying to process one critical incident, there's another around the corner, ready to trip you up psychologically yet again. Just when you think you have seen it all, something unexpected crosses your path. Trite as it is, you can't help but ask the question—what the hell is wrong with people?

A retired colleague and friend of mine who plays a large role in this story, Sgt. Wayne Voida, sent me the following letter in response to the questions I posed to him, the same that were asked of me—how does the average police officer end up in a dark state of mind, and how did you arrive there?

That's one hell of a tough question to answer. 34 years as a cop profoundly changed me, and most definitely not for the better. I would compare it to acquiring a very slow-growing and eventually fatal physical disease such as cancer, but this disease wastes away your psychological well-being.

You become desensitized and quite hardened very early in your career. You develop all sorts of dysfunctional coping mechanisms. Your daily exposure to man's inhumanity to man continues to eat away at you from the inside; you see things no human being should see, and worse yet, you do things that no human being should have to do.

Your faith in mankind is the initial casualty lost to "the job." Then, after continuous exposure to the evil and extensive corruption present in our criminal justice system, you begin to realize just how futile your efforts to help the good people truly are. Your compassion slowly dies. Your dedication to your mission slowly dies. Your sense of right and wrong becomes relative, compromised, and dependent upon the specifics of a situation. Your core principles and your fundamental beliefs are severely tested, and for some, just disappear.

As you become an experienced veteran officer, you finally reach that point where that small flickering flame of anything you clung to that represented your internal idea of goodness is extinguished. It goes out for the final time; you are irreparably damaged, and your spirit is permanently broken.

Your existence is now characterized by unending suspicion and mistrust, even with the few people who have found a way to still care about you in spite of yourself and what you have become. You are jaded, cynical, and skeptical. You are corrosively sarcastic, and your sense of humor is dark. You despise the company of strangers and actively pursue solitary activities. The only time you are anything close to comfortable is when you are isolated from all of your fellow humans. You see only the bad in everything around you, and it continues to destroy you from the inside out.

And then, as it inevitably does for us all, death comes to end your miserable existence. And even though you may have the good fortune of still having a few people in your life who have found that seemingly impossible way to feel love for you and possess the kindness to be physically present in your final moments, you still, in your own mind, die alone. You die haunted by the bitter memories, anger, and hatred that have kept you imprisoned for decades. You die alone and broken.

And there it is—the real and raw answer to those questions. Many retired police officers end up mere shadows of the optimistic rookie they once were. We devolve to view everything through the lens of race and culture, courtesy of differing political ideologies and a broken criminal justice system. At some point, the distinction between right and wrong no longer matters as long as the ends justify the means. You risk becoming the very beast you hoped to eradicate. As Friedrich Nietzsche put it, "Whoever fights monsters should see to it that in the process he does not become a monster. If you gaze long enough into an abyss, the abyss will gaze back into you."

During my nearly three-decade-long career, I've been called a heavy-handed racist by far-left camps, and a "hug-a-thug" progressive by far-right camps. In these pages, I search for the truth, which I believe exists somewhere in the middle of those two poles.

This story is born from one moment in my 28-year career—decisions made within 43 seconds of time. Yet, I hope it shows the interconnectedness and impact that two young men's actions within a moment lasting only seconds can have in this web of life.

CHAPTER 1

A DARK NIGHT'S EVE—1990

Living in fear of the unknown became my new normal the night I killed an unarmed Black man on the city streets of Indianapolis. The moment I pulled the trigger, I knew one thing for sure: my life had changed forever. Killing another human being will do that to you. The trajectory I thought I was on at that point in time morphed from a straight, defined line into the shape of a large question mark. After that night, for years, the only thought I found my mind ruminating on was—what now?

Unfortunately, I can tell you what now.

When a white police officer kills an unarmed Black man, what follows is legal battles, court trials, media frenzies, and polarized communities. He spirals into addiction, suicidal ideation, and a complete unraveling of his personal life and relationships. He begins asking the question—who am I?

But the guy who pulls the trigger never suffers as much as the one on the other end.

In the three decades that ensued since the shooting, I vacillated between searching for answers and numbing the parts of me that asked the questions. According to theories of those I studied in search for an explanation to the age-old question—why are we here—each soul starts its current incarnation with a specific focus, maybe something it needs to learn. My best guess after the copious amounts of reading and research I've done on the subject is that these theories all point to a common theme: until your soul finally gets it right, another lifetime of suffering ensues. Some souls, like mine, must be slow learners.

After the fallout of the shooting, it has taken me years to sort out what it all means, and even today, with a somewhat clearer understanding, I still don't know how all of the puzzle pieces fit. But even before that fateful night, I've had an inexplicable feeling that I was destined to meet someone in this lifetime for some specific, albeit hidden, reason. Maybe a preconceived encounter designed by the Universe to bring me a lesson, message, or a new level of understanding—a level that would take decades to unfold. What I didn't know is that this unlucky meeting would involve one of us dying, and one of us surviving.

This story takes an interesting, maybe even confusing turn when you compare the professional life I've lived with the spiritual flavor of this talk of a soul's journey. I'm a retired law enforcement officer with 28 years of service for the Indianapolis Metropolitan Police Department (formerly IPD). After graduating the police academy at the age of 23, I started my career, as many do, as a patrol officer. Still a rookie in both thought and career at that time, I had just begun my own research into spirituality and the important life questions.

My personal process of waking up was abruptly halted when life took a sharp, dark turn in July 1990. On a hot and sticky

Midwestern summer night, in the line of duty, I shot and killed a robbery suspect after a long and dramatic police pursuit. My progress down the path of a greater opening and understanding of the nature of our Universe and human consciousness was brought to a crossroads.

Vilified by many, yet eventually exonerated in federal court, my shooting was deemed a justifiable response to the circumstances presented to me when, in that split second, I chose to pull the trigger. In the years to follow, I endured much media and public scrutiny for killing a young Black man who, in the end, turned up unarmed. While I had a successful career, feeling that I made a positive contribution to the city in terms of reducing crime and initiating helpful programs, the pivotal experience has left an indelible mark on my soul.

EARLY UPBRINGING.

A self-proclaimed hopeful agnostic for most of my life, the rigidity and ritual of organized religion never rang true to me. The rules and restrictions just didn't feel right, and in fact, translated in my mind to hypocrisy and deception. I learned as a young boy that prayer didn't work, at least when I attempted to elicit help for my mom on those nights when Dad came home in a drunken rage. (As much as I wanted to grow up and be just like my dad, I made a vow to never grow up and be just like my dad.) As a frightened child, I felt powerless to stop the violence.

All I could do then was bury my head in my pillow, trying to drown out the terrifying sounds beyond my closed door, all the while hoping they didn't migrate back to my bedroom. I remember once hearing glass breaking. My parents had mirrored folding closet doors in their bedroom. On one occasion, after a night of slamming and shattering, Dad came home with a new panel to replace the one he destroyed the night before. On nights like that, I would always awaken in the morning to normalcy and Mom with an unwavering smile, serving me breakfast before school. It wasn't until years later that I realized she was the rock of our family—the one who held everything together.

In my late teens, things began to change for me internally as those violent nights unfolded, and while prayer didn't work, I learned that overt physical intervention did. Lucid and sober, my dad was the most wonderful man I'd ever known. But like all of us, he had a dark side. Stopping him in the middle of one of his drunken attacks on Mom was the first time I learned to fight for a victim—a skill that would serve me well later in my career.

My views on religion were shaped in part by my father's disdain for the hypocrisy of church dogma, and my mother's Universalist Unitarian upbringing in Creston, Ohio. Mom and Dad tried their hand at organized religion in a small-town Presbyterian church while I was still an infant, but their stint there quickly ended when news broke that the married minister of the church, who stood at the pulpit preaching chastity every Sunday, was having an affair with the funeral director's wife down the road. Religion did not have any role whatsoever in my formative years. In my twenties, I would have described myself as very spiritual, but not religious.

I started a process of "waking up" spiritually back in the late 80s. I'm not sure at the time I knew what that term meant, or was even aware of it, and it wasn't until many years later that I could have defined my experience with those words. In *Waking Up, A Seeker's Memoir*, Sam Harris, philosopher, neuroscientist, and bestselling author, acknowledges that 20 percent of Americans describe themselves as spiritual but not religious. He says although the claim annoys believers and atheists equally, separating spirituality from religion is perfectly reasonable and normal. People who claim this as their truth, according to Harris, are validating two important notions: Our world is dangerously driven by religious doctrines that all educated people should condemn, and yet there is more to understanding the human condition than science and secular culture generally admit.

Bingo. Harris articulated what rang true for me. I wondered where this guy was when I started searching for answers 32 years ago.

My life divided into two distinct categories in 1990: before the shooting and after the shooting.

Before the shooting, I was venturing into the works of the famous Carl Jung and pioneers of transpersonal thought, such as Edgar Cayce. Eventually, I delved into martial arts. As I parsed out the philosophies of each discipline, I found myself particularly drawn to those that proffered peace as a solution to conflict through body in motion, such as Aikido, (which is translated as "The Art of Peace," or "way of harmonious spirit"). I'm well aware that some hardline martial artists will call Aikido a choreographed dance, but others call it an effective system of conflict neutralization. Either way, the subject matter was incredibly evocative for me at that time. In the name of self-preservation, I eventually chose the harder-line system of Kempo as my focus. Despite the power

13

associated with the badge on my chest, I felt I was being called to use it to heal—not hurt.

Throughout 20 years on the force, I was a proud member of the SWAT team and was involved in hundreds of high-risk felony warrants, hostage situations, and dignitary protection details. If you're anything like me, once you taste the adrenaline rush of crashing through the door on a high-risk warrant, you're immediately addicted to that high. I would go on to hold positions as Entry Team Leader, Assistant SWAT Commander, and eventually, SWAT Commander, during my stint on the team.

After rising through the ranks on the force, the pinnacle of my policing career was being appointed deputy chief of operations in 2011. Not having much tolerance for desk jobs or sitting still for very long in a work environment, I maintained what I knew to be my true course. I have always considered myself a street officer through and through. Never forgetting where I came from, I carried it with me into that administrative position.

After decades of service and a successful career, albeit riddled with controversy and trauma, I am now living on the Outer Banks of North Carolina near the healing salt waters of the Atlantic Ocean. It's good for the soul here. Locals often stop what they are expected to do, like work, to enjoy life for a while. If the surf's up, the surf's up. Short of the tourists, no one seems to be in a hurry. Life here embodies a paced island mindset—one where a sign on the door reading, "No shirt, no shoes, no service," would translate to no customers. It's my kind of place where a local's bumper sticker reads, "My only friends are pirates." In this life, after years of daydreaming of moving here after retirement, it's a place I now call home. I feel like maybe I've called it home before.

It is here that I continue my spiritual seeking as I sort out the past, put the present in order, and think about the future. Back to the notion I referenced earlier of "waking up," I find it holds many meanings for those who claim it. I certainly believe in a Universal power greater than individual ego. What that is, I am not exactly sure at this point. In the way I've come to understand it, waking up is an awareness that we are all connected to everyone and everything in the Universe, yet we are all on different circuits or paths that connect directly to a source—however you choose to define or label it. Thus, hurting another is akin to self-mutilation.

It also means that we as individuals all have the potential to reach higher levels of spiritual consciousness devoid of the purported truths and corruption of organized religion. Spirituality without religion is a path anyone can take. I've always agreed with the notion that religion is for those who fear going to hell. Spirituality is for those who've already been there. It's a personal endeavor. It's achieving a sense of peace and knowing from the inside out on our path to return to our source, not having to be held by the hand and directed by some misguided theologian's profitable, cloaked dogma.

According to my good friend and spiritual advisor Annie, metamorphosis, as with any birth, starts by turning you upside down.[2] My prolonged period of spiritual stasis and dark night of the soul that commenced at the site of the shooting would last for the next 30 years of my life.

This is not a feel-good story. I wanted it to be when I started writing, but it's not. It's about a regular young man invigorated by innocence and idealism who wanted to do good. In the pursuit of making the world a better place for the future, he killed another young man who was deserving of a future. And as this was a very public death, I wrestled with the gravity of it internally while the world around me took polarized positions: One camp that cried, "Racist. Nazi. Murderer," and another that argued, "Self-defense. Good guy fights bad guy and wins." Somewhere between the juxta-position of the murder narrative and the duty and self-survival narrative lies a universal truth and understanding that I hope begins to take shape within these pages.

To a certain degree, this story is also about tribalism and the politics of division—weaponizing race against one another in which the ends-justify-the-means ideology prevails. This is also an account of a warrior ethos for those on the path of answering their own personal call to service. As is the case with many warriors, my current incarnation has seemingly been touched more by those dying than by those living.

It's about a world in which constantly living post trauma becomes your new normal.

I've found the hard way that a warrior life—the calling I honored—by its very nature, will either brew the perfect psychos-piritual storm leading to transformation, or materialize as addiction, dark and self-destructive ideation, or attempted and/or completed suicide. For me, this story is a cathartic endeavor, but also a means to connecting with warriors whom others will never understand. I often read online support forums for former military and law enforcement personnel who suffer from PTSD, and I see a recurring story line: "I was eager to serve prior to raising my right hand to support and defend our Constitution. But having seen what I've seen and done what I've done, I haven't been the same since." In the end, I hope it provides fuel for further thought and dialogue that might prove a harbinger for individual and collective healing in the future.

As I sit here all these years later, I've embarked on a brand-new chapter of my life—a sober one with healthy relationships. When I started writing, my therapist warned me, "Be extremely careful, Scott. This could be a cathartic endeavor for you, or you might just start drinking again before you finish chapter two."

During the drama immediately following the shooting, I was warned by some ranking mentors of mine on the force, "Stop watching the evening news, Scott. And cancel your newspaper subscriptions. If you don't, you'll go nuts." So this is the first time, literally, I've sat down and read these clippings that are spread here before me.

Sifting through the voluminous articles and letters generated about me, preserved meticulously by my mom, I see one that stands out. On one article of many she sent to my maternal grandmother to keep her informed of her grandson's passionately chosen, yet quickly turning tumultuous career, she wrote, "This is not the end! Have to wait on the grand jury and then tackle the [family's civil] lawsuit!! Scott ought to write a book!"

Well, Mom—here goes.

CHAPTER 2

ON SACRED GROUND

U nbeknownst to me at the time of the shooting, I was standing on what would later be proclaimed "sacred ground" as my dark journey began. Was it just plain coincidence, or a twist of fate that directed me to that intersection of 10th Street and North College Avenue? I don't know the answer yet. In time, I may.

There, for a split second in time, I seemed to briefly come out of my body and watch the events unfold beneath me, all the while having some unexplainable understanding that I would survive.

It was Monday, July 9, 1990, just several hours after midnight. There at that intersection, the perfect storm of racial divide and self-destruction sparked by this event was brewing. As the police started arriving, fragments of conversations happening around me randomly pierced through the chaos happening in my head.

"It was a good shooting, Chief," was one comment I heard clearly. It was my fellow SWAT team member, Sgt. Wayne Voida, talking to the deputy chief of operations. This oxymoron, "good shooting," was not meant to be a proverbial "high five." In police vernacular, it meant that it was completely justifiable according to departmental rules and regulations. While it felt good to hear those words in that moment, adrenaline was still coursing through my veins, and I was not processing anything well. Personally and politically, I had no idea what I had just unearthed.

Every wet-behind-the-ears police recruit contemplates "the" question, and it's a daunting one: Will I be involved in a shooting?

In police academy presentations I've facilitated since the event, I've proffered the following thought to new recruits who are answering their calling: "You don't get to choose the time and place of your future shooting. It chooses you."

With the power of death on my hip and the symbolic police badge on my chest representing the oath to serve and protect life, I reported to work one night early in my career. It was Sunday evening, July 8, 1990. Just four years prior, I graduated from the Indianapolis Police Department Academy. I still had the stainless-steel Smith and Wesson .38 special snub-nosed revolver that is customarily awarded to the officer who finished first in his or her academy class. It was now strategically positioned on my body as my last-ditch backup weapon in case I lost control of my primary duty pistol. I was 26 years old. For all intents and purposes, I was still a kid—driven by some sort of inner utopian altruism to protect and serve those in need.

My radio call-sign was Adam-346. That signified that I was assigned patrol duties on a beat located within one of several quadrants of the city, the Adam Sector, Late Shift. My hours were 9:30 p.m. to 5:30 a.m. Some in the profession call it the graveyard shift for obvious reasons.

Here in the Heartland, the annual Indiana Black Expo (IBE) was set to kick off the following week. This yearly event was founded in 1970. Its website says that Indiana Black Expo has been a pillar of the community for well over 40 years now. "It has encouraged, uplifted, and celebrated the accomplishments and achievements of African Americans throughout Indiana. Throughout various symposiums with civic leaders speaking on pressing economic, political, and social issues, IBE has strived to address past, present, and future issues that face African Americans and all people alike."[3] The site credits support and guidance of popular entertainers and political figures, such as the Rev. Jesse Jackson, Louis Farrakhan, and Kenny "Babyface" Edmonds—an Indianapolis native singer–songwriter.

The year 1990, however, was different as it marked the Expo's 20th anniversary of "Summer Celebrations," as it was frequently billed. *Jet Magazine* would later refer to this platinum celebration as, "The nation's largest event showcasing African American accomplishments."[4] All this in a state that at that time recorded one of the smallest concentrations of Black citizens in the country[5]. On the pages of the *Indianapolis Recorder*, the local African American newspaper, one writer even touted, "Some enthusiastic fans will argue that Expo is bigger than Christmas."[6]

The Rev. Jesse Jackson was the event's keynote speaker. Former Virginia Governor Doug Wilder, the nation's first African American elected to serve as a state governor since the post-Civil War Reconstruction, would be in town to accept the 1990 Freedom Award. The award was being presented to the nation's top humanitarian from Black Expo president, the Rev. Charles Williams. Oscar-winning actor Lou Gossett Jr. would receive the "Above and Beyond Award." The great Muhammad Ali and Babyface would be in town to be honored for their accomplishments, as well. The celebration featured other top name stars from the entertainment world. Janet Jackson would be performing the Rhythm Nation Tour at Market Square Arena, which has long since been demolished. The *Recorder* also boasted, "Starting the line-up are some of the hottest and best in rap music. On the bill for 'Rap Tour 90' are Heavy D and the Boyz, Public Enemy, Digital Underground, Kid n Play and EnVogue."[7]

Before leaving for work that night, I had that gut feeling officers sometimes have. That feeling is hard to explain. I knew something out-of-the-ordinary was going to happen that night.

After leaving North District roll call around 10 p.m., my partners and I, as our nightly routine dictated, went to 38th and North Keystone Avenue to enjoy conversation and our first cup of piping hot coffee at a local White Castle. After, we took a few standard radio runs. Nothing exciting. Here in the big city, it was just another boring Sunday night. Despite my gut feeling, I wondered, what could possibly go wrong? Sometime after midnight, we decided to circle the wagons back at the White Castle for more convening. Before we finished that second cup of joe, however, our conversation came to a halt.

"Attention all cars, attentions all cars. An armed robbery just occurred at the Taco Bell located at 6335 East 82nd Street," the dispatcher announced. The suspect was a Black male armed with a revolver who fled the scene of the robbery in a new red Chevrolet Camaro. According to the *Indianapolis News*, the incident began at 2:50 a.m. William Scott McBride, night manager of the Taco Bell, was locking up the business. McBride said as he finished and walked to his car, he was approached by a man who was standing next to the Camaro. The suspect, brandishing a long-barreled revolver, ordered McBride back into the restaurant and told him to open the safe. McBride said the suspect took two bank money bags, plus McBride's wallet. Before fleeing in the car, the suspect was reportedly quoted as saying, "I've killed one man tonight already."[8]

A vehicle fitting the description was stopped by Marion County Sheriff's Deputy Sgt. Michael Smith at I-70 and Shadeland Avenue at about 3:06 a.m. After approaching the vehicle for the first time, Deputy Smith obtained the operator's driver's license and registration and called for backup.

A few miles away, my academy classmate, Officer Theresa Hedge, was idling in a parking lot, about to share a mid-shift pizza with Officer Mike Knapp, when they heard the broadcast. Hedge recounted to me all these years later, "We heard that the officer had the car stopped at I-70 and Shadeland. We were just getting ready to crack that pizza, but we said, well, let's go."

Hedge and Knapp pulled onto the highway just as the license check was coming back. It was in the name of Leonard R. Barnett, Black male, 25 years old, and the sole occupant of the vehicle. Hedge remembers that as she and Knapp pulled in behind the traffic stop, she saw Smith outside of his car approaching the suspect's vehicle from the passenger side. Hedge exited her vehicle and approached the driver's side of the Camaro. As she recalls, "My first thought was—this is the armed robber? This guy's good-looking!"

She ordered Barnett to place both hands outside of the driver's door window, to which he initially complied. But then, Barnett quickly looked over to the passenger's side, where Smith was standing. He then pulled his hands back inside the window and began reaching between the driver's seat and the console. Hedge said from her point of view, she saw the suspect bring his hands together, but that was all she saw before she heard Smith yell, "Gun!"

Smith saw the gun, yelled the warning, then stepped back and fired at Barnett. Hedge fired, as well. As Barnett put the vehicle in gear and fled at a high rate of speed, all three officers jumped back into their vehicles in pursuit.

The Indianapolis News reported that during the nearly hour-long chase, police officers and sheriff's deputies exchanged several shots with Barnett on the city's Eastside. The suspect was shot and killed after his car crashed at 10th Street and College Avenue.

That's an oversimplified version of how it unfolded.

Here's Hedge's eyewitness account:

> "Smith hollers, 'Gun!' He jumps back and we both fire at the vehicle. Barnett's backup lights come on, and the car takes off. And I'm thinking, Oh shit…
>
> We all take off. Smith made it ahead of me right off the bat. Mike flies around me. I realized I was in low, not drive, so I pop it into drive then take off. I was the last one in line at that point. We get off on Emerson. By the time I get to the top of the ramp and get to 25th Street, the dust starts turning up. They had actually gotten into a parking lot, and everyone is spinning around in circles. The Camaro pulls out of it and continues southbound. He gets a little ahead of me and immediately turns right into a [newspaper] drop off point.

By the time I turn into the parking lot, he's headed at me full speed. I stop, jump out between my door and car frame. I fire one shot at his windshield. He starts to go around me on the right. I start pulling on my trigger, then saw the police lights coming, so I pulled my shot downward. The Camaro turns back northbound. It was kind of like *Keystone Cops*. Everyone is now headed back northbound to Emerson. I'm the last one up there. The radio traffic is, 'Which way did he go? Which way did he go?'

I turned south. Everyone turns off sirens and lights. I see a little old man sitting in a pick-up truck, asked him if he saw a red Camaro, and he pointed southbound. I don't see any taillights. I come up to the 21st Street Shell station, asked the guys standing out there, where did the Camaro go? They said west. I put it out on the radio, but I still didn't see any taillights. I shut it down by that point. There was no telling how many police cars were involved.

Then I hear [Sgt.] John Moore is saying, 'He's coming at me; he's coming at me!' Barnett is charging him, so he backs up out of the way. Barnett heads west on 16th Street. Moore lost him. Then [Officer] Ron Gray was kicking him up by Linwood Square, then lost him. I thought the suspect was down at Linwood and Washington. I turned off on New York Street. I pull up on Linwood and see nothing. Checked in with control. I decided to go north on Linwood. I pull over in the 900 block, smoke a cigarette, get a drink of Mountain Dew, and decide to reload.

All of a sudden, there he goes westbound on 10th Street, so I jumped out behind him and the chase was on again. There was no vehicular traffic out except for us. I got my mic in my left hand, my right hand on the steering wheel, and we're approaching downtown. He ends up hitting the curb in front of me as we went under the interstate. He was fishtailing so bad, and I was at such a high rate of speed. I hit the brakes, and then I hit on the left-hand side curb, blew a tire, and went over the median. Next thing I know, I saw the bus coming at me. I put my hand in front of my face with an, oh shit. My car is steaming. I tried to open my driver's side door—wouldn't open. I climbed out through the window. I landed on my hands and knees. Then it was nothing until I came to about 5:30 a.m. at the hospital."

The fishtailing.

That's where Hedge's story with Barnett ended and mine began.

I was hearing this on the radio traffic. It sounded absolutely crazy.

I positioned myself at East 10th Street and North College Avenue to block one-way north-bound traffic and stop motorists from traveling north bound across Barnett's path.

I saw the Camaro flying westbound underneath the interstate approaching College Avenue. He was still running dark—traveling without headlights or taillights in order to elude pursuing officers.

Not too far behind the Camaro, I also saw Hedge, the only pursuing vehicle, with overhead red lights rotating. I did not, however, see her crash into a parked school bus. I faintly heard the police siren as my adrenaline flow peaked and my heart pounded.

I saw the Camaro fishtail as Barnett lost control east of College.

At that intersection, a light pole stood along with a couple of street signs. Barnett hit the curb and ran over the light pole, flattening it just before the car became airborne. I watched in awe as the car cleared all five lanes of College and flew through the air. I never saw the vehicle's wheels touch the ground after lift-off. I watched it collide head-on into the elevated cement porch of the house on the northwest corner of 10th and College. The vehicle folded like an accordion from the force of impact. It was the most violent crash I had ever witnessed.

"10th and College, he's stacked it up bad," I screamed into my radio. "Start a medic, control," I said.

During the lengthy on-again, off-again pursuit that reportedly reached speeds in excess of 80 mph, Barnett was able to skillfully elude other officers and dodge vehicles in his path for miles. Yet somehow, he lost control there, crashing right in front of me as I sat in my police vehicle, blocking traffic.

As the Camaro cannoned into the porch coming to an instant halt, I jumped out of my vehicle and drew my weapon for protection. I wasn't taking any chances, even though I assumed from the severity of the crash that Barnett was either dead on impact or needing extensive medical treatment. I ran toward the scene to check on his welfare. My mind was racing, but my primary thoughts were, *detain immediately and provide medical assistance.*

As I ran toward the scene, I saw Barnett standing outside of the vehicle, but I never saw him get out of the car. I couldn't imagine how he managed that considering the severity of the crash. Did he open the door? Did he crawl through the window? It seemed as if he just appeared somehow there in front of me.

I aimed my pistol directly at his chest. As I looked through the sights, I ordered him—no, I screamed at the top of my lungs, "Get on the fucking ground!" He didn't hear me, wasn't listening, or was just outright disobeying my order. Staring intensely, he seemed to look not at me, but right through me with an absent gaze, and he started to run at me. In my later testimony to a grand jury, I described his seemingly rapid movements like "a track star coming out of the blocks." That statement would come back to haunt me in future court proceedings.

As he approached me, I responded as I was trained to do in a violent, up-close, and personal attack. I pulled my pistol backward toward my right hip to prevent him from seizing it. As I did this, I simultaneously hit him as hard as I possibly could with the palm of my left hand. I used enough force that he stumbled backward into the back-rear quarter panel of the Camaro. To my astonishment, he charged at me again. Aiming at his chest, I screamed, "Get on the fucking ground!" Again—he did not obey my command. He paused for a moment, looked back at the vehicle, then back at me. It occurred to me that he was sizing up his options. Incredulous, I tried to manage the chaos in my head so I could grasp for some sort of logic within what was unfolding in front of me.

I yelled, "No, don't go back to the car!"

My thoughts were racing.

Where's my fucking backup? Why isn't he listening to me?

I screamed again for a third time, "Get on the fucking ground!"

He then ran toward the Camaro and dove head-first into the driver's side window. I could only see his back and lower half at that point. I could no longer see his hands. I saw him throwing things around, as if he was searching for something. I thought I saw cash flying as he rummaged through the front seats.

Searching.

Searching for something.

Suddenly, he just stopped. It looked like his arms came together, as if he grabbed something. My immediate thought was that he located the gun he was armed with during the robbery. He glanced back until he made direct eye contact with me. He began pulling himself back out of the window.

At that moment, I thought it was him or me. I fired. In that split second, my life changed forever.

That moment seemed like an eternity.

It's hard to explain the situation from there. It's an experience that doesn't even make sense to me. I didn't then, nor do I now recall ever having pulled the trigger on my pistol. Yet, I indisputably did. I never heard or felt the weapon discharge.

In the academy, I learned that in a life or death, fight-or-flight encounter, in addition to potential loss of hearing awareness, the involved officer could also lose fine motor skills. Tunnel vision is often reported as you focus in on what matters at that time—the suspect's hands. "Always remember," academy and firearm instructors implored, "it's the suspect's hands that will kill you. Don't ever lose sight of their hands." You become keenly focused on one thing and one thing only: your survival.

During my encounter with Barnett, I began to experience time in still frames and slow motion. Yet somehow, all movement within each frame seemed rapid. In that split second that I pulled the trigger, I was aware of being outside of my own body, seemingly detached or dissociated from it.

Within that second, it seemed, I was both observer and the observed.

I was only aware I had fired when I noticed the smoke from the discharge of the firearm as it eerily raised skyward, backlit by the streetlamps. As normal processing of real-time events returned to me, so too did my hearing. I could hear things again that I didn't just seconds before, like the sirens of all responding vehicles. Soon after firing the shots, I heard police radio traffic again. I watched as Barnett seemed to slowly make his way to the ground. Coming out of that ultra-focused state, I got on my radio.

"Control, shots fired. I need… I've got to have help here immediately, and I need one of our supervisors."

I heard the dispatch operator announce, "All cars, officer down at 10th and College."

"Adam-346 to control," I screeched like a boy in puberty. "I'm fine, but I need a medic down here for this clown." Another statement that would haunt me in the future.

It was finally over.

I was still alive.

Barnett was now on the ground in front of me.

The first responding officers, Steve Kincade, Wallace Shobe, and Jeff Avington arrived almost immediately after Barnett started going down. I watched as Shobe and Kincade handcuffed him. It looked like he was still fighting.

How is he still fighting? I must have missed him, I thought.

As Avington recalled decades later, "I saw you covering the other guys as they handcuffed him. It looked like they had him under control, so I approached·you."

As he came closer, I remember hearing Avington say something to me about a gun. I couldn't figure out why he seemed to get taller and shorter with every passing second. I found out later I was jumping up and down from the adrenaline dump.

The gun, he kept saying.

How is there still a gun, have I missed someone else who's armed? I began scanning for another suspect.

Avington remembers that as I jumped, I said, "I shot him. I shot him. I think I missed." He said he looked back at Kincade and Shobe struggling with Barnett and thought maybe I was right. I missed. "But then I saw his shirt turning red with blood," he said.

It finally registered that the gun Avington was talking about was mine. He was telling me to calm down and holster my gun, which I was still pointing in the direction of the handcuffing officers. They didn't need cover anymore. It was all over. "You didn't do anything wrong," Avington remembers telling me.

The scene seemed ridiculously chaotic now. That split-second feeling of an external guided control over fear disappeared. Officers were still responding at lightning speed to provide backup. The sound of sirens was deafening. It was then I knew what I had just done.

Later in my career, I was asked to run through this shooting with academy recruits in several classes. I presented it as a role-playing scenario, walking them through each moment of the encounter and asking them to stand in my shoes on that night. I would finish with, "You see his hands come together, and he turns toward you as he comes out of the vehicle. What do you do? Raise your hand if you'd shoot." Most of the recruits raised a hand. A few people said they wouldn't have shot.

Someone answered, "Sir, I don't know what I'd do."

That's the most honest answer anyone could give. You won't know the answer until it's over.

After having been stripped of my pistol, which would now be considered evidence, I was placed in the back seat of a police car, like any suspect would have been. Sgt. Wayne Voida eventually got in the car with me. He was sent as a representative of the POST (Police Officer Support Team) that had recently been formed to respond to post-trauma incidents involving police officers. Looking back on the incident now, Voida says I was in psychological shock. "You were surprised, stunned, and had an expression on your face like, 'What the fuck just happened?' Almost in a state of disbelief," he said.

I sat in the car as a whirlwind of police activity surrounded me: lights, sirens, officers pacing, racing, talking into their radios. And I was the epicenter of the madness. My legs bounced incessantly. Voida just sat with me.

He asked, "Are you ok?"

"Yes. I told him not to go back to the car. I told him to get down."

He kept reassuring me without pressing for more information.

"You're ok. You're ok. You did what you had to do to make it home to your family safely. Good job," he said.

As I sat there waiting, I made one phone call. I called Tammy, my wife at the time, to tell her what happened. From her recollection, I was using a car phone. I said I'd be home late because I had just shot someone.

She said, "Are you ok?"

"Yes," I said.

"Is the person ok?"

I said, "Tam, I don't think so. He's on his way to the hospital. I don't think he's going to make it."

She called my parents so they wouldn't wake up to news reports of a shooting involving their son. She started the conversation with, "Scott's ok, but…"

It was one of those late-night/early-morning phone calls that loved ones of public safety personnel dread answering.

Tammy continued, "He shot someone."

After collecting his thoughts, my dad wanted to know, "Is the suspect dead?" And then, "Was the suspect Black?" He instinctively knew that an affirmative answer to both questions—even without all the facts—poses a whole different dynamic for white police officers responding with deadly force. This was as true three decades ago as it is in today's even more divisive political climate.

Following an officer-involved shooting, it was departmental policy and practice at that time to take the officer's statement as soon as possible after the scene was stabilized. Regardless of what the officer might be going through emotionally and psychologically, it was the detective's responsibility to conduct business as usual.

I was transported to the homicide office at the Indianapolis Police Department (IPD) headquarters. There, my initial statement was taken by homicide detective Sgt. Dave Phillips and witnessed by Sgt. Mark Prater and Sgt. Charles Briley. (Briley would later be assigned as the case agent.) Even today, when reading the typed transcript of my sworn statement, my heart rate quickens, my breathing labors, and my pulse throbs. My anxiety must have been ten-fold at the time.

My statement began at 6:27 a.m., just a few hours after the shooting and nearly a day since I had last slept. Because of our sleep cycle, late shift officers are normally walking zombies in daytime hours. To compel an officer's statement in this condition, let alone after a shooting, is not optimal, to say the least. As Sgt. Voida noted, I was in a state of shock. The statement I was about to make could be used against me in court and/or determine my future employment.

I would soon be viewed as the accused, a future defendant.

I had just killed somebody's son.

CHAPTER 3

TRUTHS AND CONSPIRACIES

T he fundamental truths that began to surface in the days following the shooting were more significant and overwhelming than what could have been penned by a fiction writer.

Truth One: I had just killed Leonard Barnett, an unarmed Black male, in the week leading up to the kick-off of Black Expo festivities with two-time presidential candidate Rev. Jesse Jackson due in town.

Truth Two: I shot Barnett five times with the department's first deployed for-test-and-evaluation semi-automatic Sig Sauer 9mm service pistol. The firearms staff was considering changing from the Smith and Wesson .357 magnum six-shooters for the higher capacity 9mms to keep up with the quickly evolving firearm technology in the hands of criminals. This change in weapons in that era was not without a controversy of its own.

Truth Three: The weapon Barnett used in the robbery to threaten the victim, and seen by the stopping officer, was never located by investigators.

Truth Four: I learned, to my astonishment, that Barnett had somehow managed to get out of the crashed Camaro that night and move about in front of me despite sustaining a severe open-avulsed compound "tib-fib" fracture to his lower right leg.

As Indianapolis natives and race fans might appreciate for comparison, I was told this injury was not unlike those suffered by some drivers at the Indianapolis 500. It was described to me in layman's terms that the force generated from such a high-speed, head-on collision causes the driver's legs to be forced back and upward. This acute energy cannot be withstood by the body, and the compression causes an avulsion—or pulling or tearing away—forcing the twisting bone to snap and tear through the skin, exposing the fractured bones to the naked eye.

For Barnett, the injury occurred where the ends of the tibia and fibula connect to the ankle, leaving the foot connected only by internal tissue and skin. He would have most likely been walking on the exposed bones of his right leg, which would have been in direct contact with the pavement. In future trials, this evidence would seem to contradict the statement I made that he ran at me, "Like a track star coming out of the blocks."

With those four truths cemented and immutable, even if other still-to-come details of the shooting could be disputed or questioned, my fate was determined. My 15 minutes of fame, or infamy, and the corresponding media circus had begun.

I don't remember much of that morning after I finished my statement at homicide. I made it home eventually. I was on the down slope, heading into pure exhaustion. Tammy said she'd been up the rest of the night waiting for me so she could make sure I was ok and help me through whatever I was feeling. She was very emotional and remembers being worried about me and fearful of what was to come.

The details in my mind of my emotional state are fuzzy at best, and if I had to guess, I would've told you I was a train wreck. "You weren't a train wreck," Tammy assures me. "You had a lot of adrenaline flowing. We just chatted; you told me the whole story, went through everything that happened. You were still very hyped up from everything." I had the next few days off, so we used them to stay home together, regroup, and prepare.

I was told I would be reassigned to "desk-duty," as was the department's policy after an officer-involved shooting. However, it was not desk duty per se. I was moved to the firearms section of the department's training academy. Its function was to train new recruits and in-service officers in shooting and tactics. The irony of this was not lost on me.

The department's thought process went something like this: I was a trained SWAT operator whose firearms skills might be useful in training others. Also, the range's physical location was somewhat remote, at least by urban standards. By vehicle, there was only one way in and one way out through a narrow, gated entrance. There, I would be isolated from the inevitable media onslaught.

Isolation and self-medication quickly became my two best friends—my new normal.

Fortunately, most police officers will never know what it feels like to shoot, let alone kill, another human being. On the first day of my new assignment, the range master said, "Welcome to the club. Few of us know what it's like. Now you're one of them." He wasn't implying it in an honorary or derogatory way. "Like it or not, it is what it is," he said. He warned that most people, including other officers who have never been in a shooting, may not know what to say. They may avoid the conversation all together or talk around it. He also warned that people would say extremely awkward and insensitive things, thinking they were helping. He was right.

"This one could get ugly," one of my immediate supervisors predicted. He instructed me to go down to the Fraternal Order of Police (FOP) as soon as possible and request legal assistance. As an active member, I was eligible to apply for representation for actions taken in the line of duty. After almost immediate approval on the spot, I was scheduled to meet with representatives of the FOP's go-to law firm of John C. Ruckelshaus II, or "Ruck," as he was called.

There, in my first meeting with what would become my legal team, I met Ruck. He introduced me to a young, right-out-of-law-school-looking attorney. His name was John Kautzman.

My first impression was—great. I get the new guy.

In that first of many legal defense meetings, I remember discussing what happened during the shooting.

I learned that while John may have looked like a recent law school grad, this wasn't his first rodeo. He was, in fact, some kind of legal prodigy and knew exactly what he was doing.

The media coverage of the incident started innocently enough. On the day of the shooting, the newspaper ran a photo of the crashed car with a standard article stating the known facts of the incident at that time: police shot and killed a robbery suspect after a highspeed chase.

The next day, however, media outlets, community leaders, and social justice warriors began launching a full-blown assault on the IPD and me. My supervisor's warning about this getting ugly seemed like the understatement of a lifetime. The court of public opinion was officially in session. Conspiracy theories abounded. *The Indianapolis Star* got the ball rolling innocently enough: Barnett had no prior criminal history, they acknowledged, and was gainfully employed as a manager at Indy Club Body, 620 N. Capitol Avenue—a private men's club. Officials at the club declined to comment.[9]

The *Recorder* reported that after interviewing the robbery victim, William Scott McBride, for several hours, sheriff's investigators said they were looking into the possibility of the robbery being an "inside job." One potential contributing factor: "The manager at the Taco Bell which Barnett allegedly robbed could not positively identify him from six photos displayed by police."[10] A separate article read, "Although McBride was fired for disobeying policy prohibiting employees from being alone in the restaurant, he has not been implicated in the robbery, said Sheriff's spokesman Scott Minier."[11] McBride apparently left town and could not be located for any further comment. This article, along with McBride's disappearance, began casting a shadow of doubt as alternate spins on the story surfaced.

The day after the shooting, *The Star* was the first to mention the weapon I used, calling to light the issues surrounding the department's impending change in the police-issued pistol. "Marion County Chief Deputy Coroner Charles W. Green said an autopsy showed Barnett was hit five times—twice in the chest, in the stomach, right hand, and left forearm. He was taken to Wishard [Hospital], where he died at 4:15 [am]. Barnett also fractured his right ankle during the accident. Green said it appeared the bullets that struck Barnett all came from Haslar's 9mm automatic handgun. It was the first time an IPD officer has used a 9mm handgun in a fatal shooting. The weapon is being tested as a replacement for the IPD's standard .357 caliber Magnum pistols."[12]

With the seeds of controversy planted, the *Recorder* threw the first punch. A staff writer proposed further assumptions on the validity of my report of the shooting based on the coroner's input. According to the coroner, "Barnett sustained a severe open fracture to his right ankle in the crash... He would not have been running anywhere."[13] The reporter said Barnett died from at least one of the bullets I fired that entered his left side, proceeded into his chest, and eventually tore through his heart. She also wrote that at least 18 shots had been fired by officers at Barnett during the lengthy pursuit.

Soon community leaders began calling me and the IPD on the carpet with bold claims, questioning my need to have fired my weapon at all. Michael L. Gradison, executive director of the Indiana Civil Liberties Union and cochairman of the Indiana Law Enforcement Community Relations Commission at that time, issued the following statement: "This incident points out the glaring weaknesses in our law enforcement. That was the biggest debacle involving the police department in recent memory. Why a change in weapons? We have said over and over again that the 'rapid firing' 9 millimeter weapon is useless in live apprehensions. You have to shoot them a lot more times in stopping people than you would with, let's say, a .357 Magnum. I've never heard of 23 shots fired against one person. It's still a very unfortunate occurrence and a weak contention by the police department. This is the craziest thing I've ever seen. I mean, he (Haslar) had his hands on him, for God sakes. It certainly raises some suspicions. Once again, a young Black man ends up dead and there are a lot of questions."[14]

Later, Gradison clouded the story further with a seemingly contradictory statement about the weapon in question. He told the *Recorder*, "FBI reports indicate that only one shot is needed to bring a person down when a 9mm semi-automatic pistol is fired."[15] He then continued speaking out against the actions I took in the incident. "It's just so highly improbable, the police version of what happened. It's not surprising that Barnett ran, because Black people run all the time from police—because they know what happens when you catch them. Leonard Barnett found out the hard way. Why did they have to go after him when they had his operator's license, his car registration and his license plate number? The damage to his [right] foot was far more serious than a compound fracture, and therefore there is no way he could have threatened the officer."[16]

I began to understand why my co-workers warned me against following the local news. The number of shots fired went from 18 to 23, Barnett could not have possibly walked nor posed any threat to me, and experts said that a 9mm handgun is considered useless in live apprehensions. My head was spinning.

And that was only print media.

The speculations, inaccuracies, and inconsistencies were also represented in television news reports. It seemed I was the top story every night in those first few weeks, and I was always hearing something shocking and confusing about the incident. I began to question my sanity, wondering if I was actually involved in the same incident that the news outlets were covering.

The voice of one of my first and most loyal supporters, my dad, came a few days later in written form. He sent a letter to the editor of *The Star* dated July 13, 1990. It was published a few days later:

Dear Editor:

As we continue to probe throughout the days following the Police Action Shooting of July 9, 1990, several important points concern me. The young man who was shot did more to influence that outcome than anyone else in this world. He made the decision to rob the business establishment (and from what we know today, was armed with a handgun). He made the decision to flee from police after being stopped by them. He made the decision to lead them on a high-speed chase that injured one officer and could have injured other unsuspecting citizens. He made the decision not to obey the officer who told him to lay down, and instead returned to his car still acting irrationally. This young man created this string of events, not the police or the policeman, who were doing their jobs and risking their lives to protect the decent people of our city. Now this young man is being called a "good boy?" Does this sound like a good boy to you?

The other area of concern I have are the "Do Good" groups that immediately show up on television and in the press wanting to blame the police who are simply doing their job rather than the person who committed the crime. If these groups did as much to help young people develop values and responsibilities early in their life as they do to lash out at police after an incident, we all would be better off. I for one am tired of hearing about murders, robberies and rapes, and the perpetrators of these crimes painted as "Good Boys."

Finally, I urge anyone reading this letter who is also tired of these type events, to write your local police, your Congressman or State Representative and let them know your opinion. The decent people have a voice too, let's hear from them as well as the Do-Good Groups.

A concerned citizen and father,

L.L. Haslar

This would be the first of many letters of support my dad wrote on my behalf in the following three years. A manager at one of the most lucrative Sears Roebuck department stores in the Midwest, he didn't shy away from taking a public stance in defense of his son. Every morning when he arrived at his office, his secretary had his coffee, a cigarette, and the morning newspaper waiting for him. After he read and digested the latest reports about the shooting, he put pen to paper and wrote voraciously on my behalf, his secretary later typing each letter that he would hand-sign and mail.

The same day my father's letter was dated, a significant pundit criticized the incident, offering his opinions and theories. Richard Waples, legal counsel for the Indiana Civil Liberties Union, issued his first statement. In an article on July 13, Waples initially conceded that I may have been justified in believing Barnett was still armed after the robbery. However, he claimed I violated departmental rules by confronting Barnett after he emerged from the vehicle.

"The thing that the officer is supposed to do is stay behind cover, with his gun drawn. That way the officer is not in danger of being shot at. All the police training is to minimize these types of incidents and put the person under control without exposing the officer to danger, and that wasn't followed in this case."[17] Barnett's family would eventually hire Waples to begin proceedings for a civil lawsuit against me.

In a polar extreme response to my critics, *Indianapolis News* columnist Richard K. Shull, who wrote a nationally syndicated weekly column, added his inflammatory commentary to the mix.

"Time was, if a stick-up man got himself killed in a work-related accident, it was written off as an occupational hazard and quickly forgotten. But anymore, a fatal shooting by the police is not a solution, but the beginning of a lot of questions. There doesn't seem to be anything like, as they say in sport hunting, a clean kill. It's all controversy... Patrolman Scott Haslar, a four-year policeman and believed to be the last to have fired on Barnett after the suspect was out of his crashed car, is presumed to be the one who administered the *coup de grace* with a 9mm semi-automatic weapon... So what Haslar had when he confronted the wrecked 1990 Camaro was the belief that the occupant was an armed and dangerous fleeing felon. That, most reasonable people would concede, was a strong inducement for Haslar to rat-a-tat-tat on the man who emerged... Monday morning quarterbacks on the case suggest Haslar didn't follow procedure; that he should have taken cover with gun drawn until the suspect surrendered or other police arrived to assist. But they weren't there in the heat of battle. Haslar was."[18]

He concluded by addressing the 9mm versus .357 Magnum controversy and police use of force. In his view:

"A .357 can blow an adversary off his feet, but the rapid-fire 9mm semi-automatic can subdivide him... A can of mace would be sufficient in dealing with abortion protestors, and a paint-pellet gun would adequately mark purse grabbers for future identification. The handy old police .38-caliber revolver is sufficient to deal with a mugger, and the .357 Magnum seems like gun enough to stop a holdup man. And about flag desecraters: That's what AK-47s are for."[19]

Shull may have been trying to help me, but his absurdist logic and weaponry lesson wouldn't win me any support.

By the end of the week, and just prior to official opening ceremonies for Indiana Black Expo, community leaders were calling for an independent review, the chief's resignation, and of course, my firing. Gradison implored that an independent investigation happen. "Evidence can be compromised. The combined story of IPD and the county [sheriff's department] have a lot of holes in it."[20] It was the right move, he added, that the FBI would conduct its own investigation. Arthur Jordan, education committee chairman in the local chapter of the National Association for the Advancement of Colored People (NAACP), added, "We've had a number of questionable shootings, always African American males, always by white police officers who say they were in fear of their lives. It's the same pattern and I think this community's got to look at that."[21]

Adding fuel to the racial fire, in an article with the headline, "Dirty Harry of Indianapolis Not Afraid to Fire," a writer for *The Star* interviewed Deputy Smith—the first officer to stop Barnett. (Dirty Harry refers to the iconic 1970s San Francisco homicide detective made famous by Clint Eastwood. In the movie, he carried *the* .44 Magnum Smith and Wesson revolver. He was a "shoot 'em all and let God sort 'em out" kind of police officer.) Smith said, "I'm kind of like the Dirty Harry of Indianapolis. It is just my ability to be where the crime is. It's like a sixth sense... to catch the major felons."[22]

The article said Smith fired his weapon in the line of duty nine times between July 15, 1976, and July 9, 1990. That was more than any other deputy on the sheriff's department. "I'm not prejudiced," Smith said. "I've met a lot of very nice Black people even when they have gotten caught doing something. I'm more apt to give them just a warning. People dictate a lot of what we do to them. I'm not trigger-happy. I only respond to the situation. I don't make the situations."[23] The racial chasm the incident was inciting widened.

It wasn't long before Rev. Jesse Jackson weighed in on the tragedy. On the morning of Monday, July 16, a vigil had been arranged at the intersection of 10th Street and College Avenue, where more than 100 people and the media en masse descended. At the site of my shooting, a *Star* photographer memorialized the moment in photo. The caption read, "The Rev. Jesse Jackson, Mary Booker, mother of slain robbery suspect Leonard Barnett and community activist Muhammad Siddeeq pray at the site of Barnett's death."[24] Siddeeq was a science teacher at the local inner city school John Marshal Junior High. In his younger days, he was the right-hand man of Louis Farrakhan Sr. Later, he disassociated himself because of Farrakhan's violent views.

Jackson said at the vigil, "Whenever these acts of racial violence occur—when police kill citizens, when citizens kill police—there must be a sense of outrage. We must see the value of every human life. There must be some sense of moral outrage by all people who care, beyond race and sex and religion… People who care must stand up and speak out." The community needed to reach out, he implored, "to the humble masses, the caring people and to this mother, [and] ask the community to come forward, white and Black. This killing should not divide the community; it should bring it together. This killing challenges every church leader, every denomination. Those who believe in life, liberty, the pursuit of happiness, due process and justice must come forward."[25]

During that same protest, Siddeeq added, "The police in Indianapolis have a conspiracy to kill Black men."[26] The Rev. Wayne T. Harris of Mount Olive Missionary Baptist Church called for the police chief's resignation. According to Harris, Chief Paul Annee's message to his officers was, "You can kill, and we will stand behind you."[27]

"I don't believe my son drew a gun on anyone,"[28] said Mary Booker at the vigil site. She added that the last time she would ever see her son was at a recent Sunday barbeque she attended at his invitation.

Now she stood on "sacred ground"—at the site of his death. That's what Rev. Jackson declared that intersection of 10th and College, where I shot and killed Leonard Barnett.

I will never be sure what his motivation was for using that particular term. Was it a reference to the Holy Land? Was he perhaps drawing a parallel to the crucifixion of Jesus? Or was it a term Jackson used when referring to someone of his race losing his or her life at the hands of a police officer?

Regardless of his intention, that term now holds its own meaning for me. As I look back on that shooting and the events that unfolded for decades after, I realize that intersection, for me, is where the divide began—before the shooting and after the shooting. It's where I began to question my own consciousness. Why did I seem to come out of my body the exact moment before I fired my weapon? Was it a divine plan that led me to that intersection of sacred ground?

Later that evening after the protest, Black Expo's festivities were launched, including opening ceremonies and other scheduled events with Jackson. He was already chosen as keynote speaker for the Expo's Ecumenical Service at Light of the World Christian Church. This would include a candlelight vigil with then Indiana Governor Evan Bayh, his wife Susan, and 2,500 participants, including Muhammad Siddeeq, as reported in *Jet* Magazine. Other Black ministers attended with Jackson to voice what seemed to me their beliefs that police officers were wantonly shooting young Black men in Indianapolis and throughout the country.

At a press conference about an upcoming "safe-streets" initiative, Chief Annee was ambushed about my shooting. He said, "I didn't come here to talk about the shooting, and I'll just say one more comment about that. The officer shot a fleeing armed holdup man. Call it what you want. You can sit and make judgments about whether that should or should not have occurred, but you cannot remove the fact this young man was fleeing the police, had put a gun to a man's head and robbed him of $1,200. That happened... And the officer was dealing with that dynamic at the time he confronted him. And in the calmness of rooms and offices and everything, you can make all kinds of judgments about whether that's proper or improper. But that officer made that decision in a split second based on the dynamics of that, and to judge that in any other fashion is unfair and wrong."[29]

Not including television news, that was just a fraction of media exposure in the first few weeks after the shooting.

The four-term republican Mayor William H. Hudnut III, still the longest serving mayor in Indianapolis' history, weighed in. "The cities are where justice is trampled and goodness is undercut,"[30] he said to a mostly Black Baptist congregation about the death of Leonard Barnett.[31] "Indianapolis can be like the New Jerusalem— transformed from a city where goodness is crucified to a city where goodness is put on the throne."[32] He continued, "If you and I are going to be good Christians, we have got to care about this city.[33] I know some people are upset over the police-action shooting... but it's in the hands of the FBI and the Justice Department, and we hope truth and justice will be served."[34]

In addition to my family, most of my support came from fellow officers, although that was also divided amongst racial lines, and private citizens. A somewhat conservative voice of reason that my dad listened to regularly even before my shooting was Fred Heckman, local radio host on WIBC 1070 AM. In back-to-back commentaries on July 17 and 18, Heckman mediated from a stance of common sense and common ground. I've included pertinent excerpts.

"Why have some reporters and community members felt such unease with the Leonard Barnett story? One reason certainly is because it doesn't make sense. A nice church-going guy goes crazy one night, sticks up a Taco Bell at gunpoint, leads police on a high-speed chase and is shot to death after threatening a policeman. But that's the way it is in the real world. Life doesn't always make a lot of sense, and we've forgotten that in the Leonard Barnett case.

Certain segments are trying to turn Leonard Barnett into a martyr. Jesse Jackson called the place where Barnett wrecked his car and died, 'Sacred Ground.' Barnett's mother claims evidence didn't turn up until she started talking about a lawsuit.

Let's be absolutely clear about this. Leonard Barnett held a gun on a restaurant manager, drove off with $2,000 in cash, led police on a dangerous chase through Eastside neighborhoods, may have shot at pursuing officers, wrecked his car and died while refusing to surrender and possibly threatening Officer Scott Haslar.

The evidence Mary Booker claims was planted by officers trying to frame her son was actually discovered at the time of the shooting and publicly released within twelve hours of the incident. Yet she refuses to speculate that perhaps her son played a role in exacerbating the situation and setting up his own fatal confrontation with Officer Haslar. But, as we speak in these terms, we must grieve with this mother over the loss of her child. It has to be painful to any mother but, Mrs. Booker claims Officer Haslar exceeded his authority in attempting to apprehend a fleeing armed felon and used excessive force when he thought Barnett was going for a gun. Haslar is a four-year IPD veteran and member of the SWAT Team that has not taken a life in more than one hundred call-ups. The evidence indicates that Haslar is more highly trained than the typical street patrolman or woman and, as indicated by his performance on the SWAT Team, perhaps even more judicious in his use of deadly force than other officers would be.

Critics complain that it took five shots from Haslar's 9-millimeter semi-automatic handgun to stop Leonard Barnett. Are these the same critics who complained that the more powerful .357 Magnum Haslar used to carry, packed such a charge that it had the potential to blast through a suspect and into an innocent bystander nearby and therefore an irresponsible weapon with which to arm Indianapolis Police?

The investigators, on the events of July 9, have the luxury of something Officer Haslar and his colleagues didn't have, the time for thoughtful reflection and sober assessment. At times, members of all three Monday morning quarterbacking groups have fallen short and failed to give us their best in sorting out this tragedy.

Investigators delivered details to reporters in a piecemeal fashion, stretching out over days the type of information that could have been responsibly divulged within 36 hours. Providing a more coherent, logical dispensation of the details would have pre-empted many of the questions reporters had to wait days to have answered.

During those days, there was a vacuum, into which some reporters leapt, trading fact finding for supposition and indirect questions without properly seeking answers or attempting to put doubts into proper perspective. A TV reporter runs a videotape showing Leonard's body was moved seven feet away from where he was shot. But, she never directly confronts investigators with her question, or shows them the tape and ask for an explanation. Instead, she unveils the tape at six and eleven and pronounces it to be an unanswered mystery.

The same reporter the next day claims a sheriff's deputy has given conflicting statements about his position relative to Barnett's car and she raises doubts about the lawman's ability to spot the robber's gun. Yet, the deputy actually gave only one statement. It was merely interpreted differently by two sheriff's officials. And, considering the style of car Barnett was driving, both statements can be construed as accurate. But this reporter announces it is yet another discrepancy in this case, throwing doubt on police accounts. In reality, it is nothing more than sloppy reporting and failing to put information in its proper context.

An *Indianapolis Star* account of Mayor Hudnut's call for racial harmony in the wake of the shooting refers to Leonard Barnett as 'an unarmed robbery suspect.' What the article fails to mention is that Barnett was actually an armed robbery suspect who police believe tosses his gun away during a high-speed chase.

Which brings us to this story's impact on the community. So called 'community leaders' and watch dog groups have called for outside investigators to probe the case. As a rule, the FBI typically investigates all police action shootings. One member of the Indianapolis Law Enforcement/Community Relations Coalition has said that, based on the information that was available to him at the time, Officer Scott Haslar had a legitimate reason to fear for his life. But others like City-County Councilman Glenn Howard have raised the specter of police racism. 'Another case of an African American killed by a white police officer who thought he was reaching for a gun,' says the councilman. But fellow City-County Councilman Ray Irvin hit the nail on the head last week when he said, 'Maybe the problem isn't with the police officer, but with a segment of our community that has armed itself and often turned its weapons on itself.'

We all have some soul searching to do regarding our work on and opinions about the Leonard Barnett shooting. From the police to the reporters to the community, we should all be asking, has the work of myself and my colleagues been complete, fair, and responsible? Tomorrow I'll talk about the making of a martyr and a police chief on a tightrope."[35]

Heckman's opinion about the incident was the first I'd heard that matched my perspective on what happened that night. It was as if he channeled my thoughts, questions, and confusion surrounding the claims and accusations against me and put them into words.

While I did begin to see some public support of my actions, the social justice warriors' campaign to prove I was a racist murderer

53

was picking up steam. In his police beat column, *Recorder* reporter William Alexander used his media platform to sully my name.

"Boy am I upset over the five-shot slaying of a 25-year-old Black man by Indianapolis police officer Scott L. Haslar. This is really one of the most insensitive shootings that I have seen in all of my years on the police beat and as a reporter, period. To shoot a man unarmed and unable to really move puts a lot of fear into my heart about some of these young police officers who give the appearance of shooting just to be shooting. From some of the television footage, the young man was at least eight feet from his vehicle, with a broken ankle and was not really a threat to the police officer who apparently just walked up on him and started shooting. In my eyesight, this was a highly questionable act and not self-defense as the officer would have his superiors believe. It is strange that when a white police officer kills a Black, it seems that he is always rewarded in some way by either promotion or a pat on the back for a good job, and why, I really don't know. Blacks are like sitting ducks waiting to be fired on by some young trigger-happy cop like Scott Haslar...[36] Mark my words, this kid will get jammed up again, and soon."

The letters, editorials, and commentaries continued and became increasingly incendiary. The two sides in this argument had clearly been established along racial and political lines. In the ensuing years, the events unfolded around this shooting in what looked like a theatrical production, except it was real life, not a stage.

A man was dead, and my future was on the line.

CHAPTER 4

CONCERNED CLERGY CRUSADE

The next several months entailed formal incident reviews, an FBI investigation, citizen complaints, and protests on the city streets. The public had a front seat to it all via print and TV news. And because Jesse Jackson's name was attached to the backlash, the shooting garnered national media coverage as well as local. The *Associated Press* picked up the story. Friends and family in Chicago, and some in Florida, were seeing it all unfold in their local news.

Nothing about this part of my life felt like, "This too shall pass."

I was constantly vigilant, and it was exhausting.

While the IPD got their ducks in a row to launch their internal investigations and inquiries, Leonard Barnett's family, along with a group known as the Concerned Clergy, began their very public process of lambasting the incident. The group was a grass roots committee headed by local Black church leaders whose genesis was fueled by the vigil Rev. Jesse Jackson organized at the site of the shooting.

On July 18, Barnett's mother, Mary Booker, filed a formal excessive force complaint with the newly formed Citizen's Police Complaint Review Board, which is an independent body that investigates citizens' complaints against sworn police officers. She was quoted in *The Star* as saying, "I would like to say that my son was shot in his left hand. This to my conclusion tells me that he might have begged for his life. My son had a compound fracture. This tells me that there is no way he could have walked. Anyone with a compound fracture cannot walk at all. I just hate the way everything happened. And why was he shot so many times... What happened should be accounted for."[37]

As Barnett's family and the Concerned Clergy remained vocal and gained momentum, the IPD's investigation began. The first step for a police-action shooting at that time was the in-house Firearms Review Board. This is an administrative process that's launched in the event of a "reported discharge" of a firearm by any sworn officer, not including discharges related to police training, which occur daily. This review is part of the department's general orders or written directives that tell police officers exactly how to conduct daily business. General orders include everything from how to tow a vehicle to the use of deadly force.

Back in 1990, the IPD's Firearms Review Board consisted of five members of the department, including Homicide Section commander, Training Section commander, Internal Affairs Section commander, a lieutenant or above from the district level, and a peer officer. The highest-ranking member of those listed serves as the board chairman.[38] Of the five members who sat on my review board, three of them were the highest-ranking Black administrators on the department at that time.

I was required by general orders to directly testify before the board, but I was not reluctant. I saw it as the first chance I had with a clear mind to explain what happened from my point of view. I was eager to get my side of the story on record.

I don't remember much of that testimony, but I do know that I was incredibly nervous. I knew that if the board came back and said I'd violated general orders, that it was not a "good shooting," then everything to follow would surely be uphill. I could be criminally indicted. I felt like I was talking a hundred miles an hour as I explained the incident to the group gathered in the chief's conference room that day.

On July 23, *The Star* reported, "The Indianapolis Police Firearms Review Board ruled [unanimously] Monday night that four city police officers were justified in firing shots and killing a robbery suspect."[39] I don't remember where I was or who alerted me when the ruling came out, but I do remember feeling relief at hearing the result. Captain Robert Turner, one of the Black members of the review board, spoke to the media regarding the shooting and the board's decision. Of my use of deadly force, Turner said I "acted reasonably." He went on to comment on the recent public backlash surrounding the incident. The article read, "Turner criticized Black ministers and activists who allege there is a conspiracy by police to kill African Americans in Indianapolis. Turner prefaced his remarks by saying he spoke as a Black man, not as a police officer." Turner continued, "Community Black leaders are not holding rallies in response to incidents where a Black man killed a little girl at the corner,"[40] he said, referring to a drive-by shooting that killed an innocent 12-year-old Black girl in a gang-style drive-by-shooting.

The Firearms Review Board ruling did not sit well with Barnett's family and the Concerned Clergy. By July 31, three full weeks after the shooting, organized weekly protests ensued. In one of the first, about 300 protestors led by "The Ministerial Brotherhood of the African American Community of Indianapolis," a group comprised of Black ministers from around the city, rallied outside of the City-County building, where IPD headquarters is located. They were there to demand the review of the shooting that Barnett's mother had requested from the Citizens Police Review Board. The board's meeting was in progress just inside.

In addition, the group also was protesting past officer-involved shootings of African Americans in Indianapolis. "The blood of Michael Taylor, Barnett, and others on this list of 23 senseless killings, cry out from the ground for some kind of vindication," their statement read.[41] "If the Berlin Wall can crumble in Germany, and Apartheid can crack in South Africa, then police murder can and must cease in Indianapolis,"[42] yelled Rev. Stacey R. Shields, pastor at Pilgrim Baptist Church. "We the African American community, like all other communities, are having problems with our youth. However, we strongly submit that this is no justification for our youth, and our youth only, to be shot down by police in senseless killings," he continued.

The Star reported, "Rev. Shields' statement also made nine demands including: the resignations of [the city's mayor] and Police Chief Paul Annee; the dismissal of Patrolman Scott L. Haslar;

dismantling of the Police Firearms Review Board; appointment of a special prosecutor to investigate the Barnett shooting; and improvements in police training procedures for dealing with citizens."[43] Shields said, "We do not intend to sit back any longer and endure, without resistance and protest, the continuation of these atrocities."[44] The *Recorder* reported that at one point during the demonstration, the ministers walked in on the review board's meeting, demanding that they be heard immediately, but the board couldn't review it at that time due to procedural policy. According to the article, while all of this was happening, the protestors outside sang several verses of the classic civil rights battle song, "We Shall Overcome."[45]

After that initial protest, Indianapolis' first Black Director of Public Safety, Joseph Shelton, responded. He said he was willing to meet with anyone at any time to discuss the facts surrounding the shooting. "Yes, he was killed," said Shelton, "And yes it was unfortunate but I would not agree that it was a senseless killing. We are dealing with emotion on the one hand and facts on the other."[46]

The Marion County Coroner's Office investigation was pending. The FBI also would be called on to review the matter for any possible civil rights violations. A.D. Pinckney, the president of the local chapter of the NAACP, said that his office was investigating the incident as well.[47]

Reverberations of cover-up conspiracy theories continued in the media, mostly generated by the Concerned Clergy. Rev. Wayne T. Harris offered the following nine questions regarding the shooting in a letter to the editor in the *Indianapolis News*:

1. If there is any truth to the story as it was reported in the July 14th edition of the *Indianapolis Recorder* that IPD officials speculated Barnett disposed of the gun during the 35-minute chase, then how could he have reached for a gun which had already been discarded?

2. Should Patrolman Haslar have shot a man who was neither facing him nor had a gun in view?

3. Could not Haslar have wounded Barnett in the leg or arm without killing him?

4. Are patrolmen taught only to kill and not to wound or otherwise disarm and disable?

5. Why was Barnett not held at bay until more backup arrived?

6. Is it plausible to think that maybe Barnett was diving back into or reaching for his car in order to protect himself or to dodge bullets which Haslar was already either firing or was about to fire at him?

7. Why was Barnett shot five times?

8. Does the firing of five shots, five separate pulls of the trigger into an unarmed man signify an act of racism and hate which resulted in Haslar assuming the combined role of judge, jury, and executioner?

9. The *Recorder* reports that Sheriff Sgt. Michael L. Smith reported Barnett reached for a gun when he was stopped at I-70 and Shadeland. The question is, 'Did Sgt. Smith ever actually see the gun?'[48]

The coroner's report was issued a few days later. *The Star* ran the story, along with a statement from Barnett's mother on the ruling. "Marion County Coroner Dennis J. Nichols ruled Thursday

[August 2] that an Indianapolis police patrolman was justified in fatally shooting a robbery suspect." The article quoted Nichols as saying, "A preponderance of the evidence I have shows Officer Haslar was justified in shooting Mr. Barnett and acted within police guidelines."[49]

Mary Booker responded to the finding, saying, "I think the coroner went along with the others instead of acting on his own findings. I don't know why he [the coroner] didn't have Officer Haslar testify. It's just a rubber stamp. It hurts me to know an innocent man got killed when Officer Haslar could have just shot him in the leg. It doesn't matter if the cop is Black or white. Right is right and wrong is wrong."[50]

The Concerned Clergy offered their response as well. "If the coroner is unable to cross-examine the officers,'" said Rev. Stephen J. Clay, pastor of Messiah Missionary Baptist Church, "it precludes him from being able to do extensive and exhaustive investigation."[51]

In response to the Concerned Clergy's public outcry, a column by Patrick J. Traub ran in *The Star*. Traub defended my actions in the shooting but pointed out the lack of a credible system to review the use of deadly force. Traub argued, "The power to take away someone's freedom, let alone a person's life is the most reviewed and second-guessed power our government has. Even after the constitutional protections of a trial by jury, the appeals and review of a death sentence penalty delay an execution for years. Such reviews ensure the government does not wrongly take a life."[52]

Traub said that the IPD and the self-appointed community activists were both to blame for the anger, pain, and frustration surrounding the incident. He was also the first to insinuate that the community activists might be propelled by a self-serving purpose in their very public reactions and protests. He continued, "Police did not find a gun in the car, providing many with an agenda that has more to do with self-aggrandizement than with a safe society. Unless there is some incredibly scandalous evidence not yet uncovered—which is highly unlikely—the patrolman acted as the vast majority of, if not the entire, police community would have... One fact alone should make the police investigation of the shooting credible. Not finding a gun—meaning the police did not 'plant' a gun to 'justify' the shooting—makes the police description of what happened credible."[53]

The next week brought another large protest march, with several more to follow. This particular one had a more dramatic tone as a wooden coffin was carried in the march, and protesters brandished signs decrying the shooting. *The Star* ran an article along with two large photos of the crowds flanked by news cameras, reporters' microphones jutting out to catch the rally cries. "About 300 people led by 24 ministers held a spirited rally in front of a gray coffin placed on the steps of Indianapolis Police Department headquarters late in the afternoon. It was the second such rally in the past week. Placards bearing the names of several Indianapolis residents killed by police or who died in police custody were placed in the coffin, while similar signs were sprinkled throughout the crowd."[54]

Marion County Prosecutor Stephen Goldsmith, who had already announced his aspirations of becoming the next mayor of Indianapolis, told reporters he was going to speed up the investigation and inquiry into the shooting because of the racial polarization it was generating. He described the racial tension in the city as some of the worst he'd ever seen in Indianapolis.

Indiana law requires a grand jury review of any fatal shooting by police but does not specify the deadline for such a review. Goldsmith denied wanting to make any kind of concessions or mediate between the community's dispute with city officials. He said he agreed to speed up the grand jury investigation because of his concerns about the racial tension. "I'm trying to do my legal job, fairly and correctly, and hope to be sensitive to the facts. I'm not sure I want to mediate anything"[55] he told *The Star.*

In the midst of the ever-growing tension and drama that continued to unfold, a newspaper reporter posed an important but controversial question—one that had been on my mind since the backlash began. It seemed it was on everyone's minds because the answer could potentially solve the riddles and mysteries that still remained woven throughout the entire incident.

On August 12, *The Star* ran an article titled, "Friends, family, city—all knew a different Barnett." Kevin Morgan asked the question that could potentially shed light on all of the opposing stories and theories that continued to swirl—who really was Leonard Barnett? If we could just get the facts of what this young man was going through, what was motivating him at the time, maybe we could put the pieces of the puzzle together and put an end to the guessing games as to how or why any of this happened.

In his investigative article, Morgan wrote, "The man you saw when you looked into the open casket depended on the Leonard Barnett you knew. Mary Booker saw someone else—Leonard, the son who would no longer be visiting her several times a week, telling her of a girlfriend named Ann."[56] According to his mother, armed robbery wasn't in his nature. "Leonard never wanted a gun. Leonard never wanted me to have a gun. I just got my purse snatched out here, and I said, 'I better get me a gun.' He talked me out of that real fast," she said.

The picture Booker painted of Leonard, a good boy who hated guns, bore no resemblance to the descriptions of him from the night of the shooting. There was no echo of Booker's son in the media photo of the crashed Camaro he died next to, bags of stolen money strewn about the scene. Morgan wrote, "In his past, they found nothing more serious than a traffic ticket." However, on July 25, 1990, *The Star* ran an article linking Barnett to a purse snatching incident that occurred two months prior to the Taco Bell holdup. In it, detective Jeremiah Sedam of the IPD is quoted as saying of Barnett, "He's not as innocent as some people think, he just never got caught."[57]

The victim of the Taco Bell robbery, William McBride, experienced that less-than-innocent Leonard Barnett. McBride told the coroner that on the night of the robbery, as Barnett held a long-barreled revolver behind his ear, "He repeatedly told me to move faster and repeatedly told me that he was gonna kill me if I didn't move faster."[58] In the initial police report, McBride also noted that Barnett threatened, "I've killed one man tonight already."

Before taking his managerial job at Club Body, Morgan wrote, Barnett worked and managed a similar fast-food restaurant, where he was a night-time manager like McBride. He left that job over discrepancies in missing bank receipts totaling around $500, according to his roommate, Brad Wisely.

A patron of Club Body and a friend of Barnett's, Randy L. Payne, knew yet another side of him. Payne told investigators he recalled seeing Barnett at the club a few weeks before his death. "I had noticed that he had gotten larger than what he had been and I asked him basically about his size. Len seemed to be getting both thicker and meatier like in the chest area, that type of thing and in the arms from when I first knew him, when I first met him like two years ago, he had picked up size."[59]

Payne admitted to having used anabolic steroids in the past and said he bought them from the same doctor that Barnett told him he purchased them from. Payne described how the drugs made him feel and how he recognized the same behavior changes in Barnett. "They made me feel really aggressive and hot-tempered, just almost to the point of being a violent person and it like just changes your whole personality is what it does. When I first met Len, he was an extremely gentle, easygoing, likeable person."[60]

Payne went on to say the last time he saw Barnett, he was, "just out in left field somewhere. He was basically the same type of person I was, just irritable to be around. I suggested steroid use to the coroner as a possible scenario for his actions."[61] (The article noted that despite toxicology reports that showed no evidence of steroid use, it was still possible he was taking them, but they didn't show up in the tests.)

Mary Booker disputed this version of Leonard Barnett. She stated his muscular build could only be attributed to his life-long hobby—body building. She said, "I bought him his first set of weights when he was 16."[62]

Morgan's article addressed rumors about the relationship between Barnett and his roommate, Brad Wisley. Club Body, where Barnett was employed as a manager, is a private, men-only gym and sauna. When asked about her son's possible homosexuality, Mary Booker replied, "In my opinion, Leonard was not like that. I know for a fact he wasn't homosexual. I don't think Brad is either. Now, Leonard wasn't the type to criticize somebody if they were. But he wasn't."[63]

When Brad Wisely spoke to investigators, there was no outright confirmation of the nature of his relationship with Barnett. He admitted to paying most of the bills for the two. Mary Booker thought two females also lived there, one being his girlfriend Ann. Wisley also acknowledged to investigators that he gave Len, as he referred to him, occasional loans for personal purchases. When asked about the gun, Wisley said the topic had come up between them a month ago. He said, "... he had just mentioned it, just you know that he thought it would be nice to have a gun for protection. I mean, the neighborhood we live in is not all that great. I was dead-set against guns, and I think he respected me on that."[64]

The article also included the account Wisley gave to investigators of the night of the robbery and shooting. He said after he cooked a quiet dinner at home for the two of them, Len asked to borrow his Camaro to visit family and check in at work. He called Wisley a few hours later to say he'd gotten a flat tire and would be home later. Wisley said he woke up around 2 a.m. distraught because Len wasn't home yet. He called the Club to check on him, but they didn't know where he was.

Wisely said an IPD policewoman knocked on his door at about 3 a.m. She asked him if he owned a 1990 Red Chevrolet Camaro. "I told her yes I did, but I said that my roommate has it, and she said that he was a suspect in an armed robbery and that she would like for me to stay in the house and keep the door locked. And she explained that they were going to kind of stake out the house and maybe he was going to return here."[65] Moments later, the policewoman returned. "She came up to the door again and told me that Len had been apprehended."[66] These were the details on record from Wisley regarding Barnett and the night of the shooting.

Mary Booker acknowledged that earlier in the day, hours before the robbery, Barnett reminded her that he was planning on quitting his job soon and moving to Washington D.C. with his roommate.

While the article couldn't deliver a final, clear answer as to why Barnett did what he did on July 9, reading it 30 years later, I'm not surprised. I know personally several people have told me that I have two completely different personalities: one when I'm in uniform, one when I'm not. The fact that Leonard Barnett presented different, seemingly opposite personalities to the people in his life makes sense to me. Doesn't everybody? (In today's social media-crazed world, I'm sure his Facebook profile would not have indicated a violent hold-up man.)

Demonstrations continued for the next several weeks. The clergy reiterated the list of demands they issued at the first rally—the resignation of the mayor and police chief, and my termination.

Mayor Hudnut remained mostly quiet throughout the chaos, but as calls continued for his resignation, he began showing signs of frustration with the community outcry as he tried to walk a political tightrope. He attempted to meet with the Concerned Clergy on several occasions to discuss matters. An *Indianapolis Star* article reported, "Hudnut has tried to meet with the Black ministers to discuss their demands—including a call that Hudnut resign—but they have refused."

The mayor voiced his exasperation. "Sometimes you get the feeling as though you're on the end of a yo-yo... It looks almost as though [the Concerned Clergy] are not serious about negotiating, that they want a kind of protracted opportunity here for demonstrating. I'm trying to hear what the concerns are out there. At the same time, I'm trying to make sure that we don't give the Police Department the impression that the community is not with them and doesn't want them to enforce law and order, because we do."[67] I felt some comfort in hearing that the mayor supported us, but in the midst of the ever-growing political firestorm, it still seemed he was trying to remain neutral, which didn't always translate as "support" to me in that emotional, confusing time.

Meanwhile, retroactive complaints about previous arrests I made, and the force I used in those arrests, started surfacing. My anxiety was already at peak level. Knowing my past performance on the force was being evaluated in the middle of this crisis compounded it. *The Indianapolis News* reported the Citizen's Complaint Review Board was considering whether or not to hear from a 15-year-old youth who claimed I had beaten him with a flashlight after he ran from me.

The article pointed out I was white, and the juvenile was Black. The suspect's statement read, "Well, he told me to lay on the ground. I just had got on my knees. I said, 'All right I'm getting down, sir,' and he just put his gun in and whipped out the flashlight, he did like this—pow… I just felt the blood when I was on the ground and they just got to kicking me…[68] Then the officers, stomped on my chest and stomach," he continued. The article also said the juvenile had contradicted his story several different times when talking to investigators.

From my recollection, after I chased the kid, he resisted arrest. I hit him when he began fighting me, but he didn't include that in his account. My attorney would later challenge the board's authority to review the case on several issues. One, the incident occurred before the board even existed. Two, the complaint from the mother of the juvenile was not verified under oath. And three, the Internal Affairs division had not made a decision on the incident, which was required by the board's own ordinance. A few months later, *The Star* reported that Marion Superior Court Judge Kenneth H. Johnson ruled that the board could not hear his complaint.

The teen was publicly identified on October 4, 1990. "A teenager whose brutality complaint against Indianapolis police led to legal challenges against the Citizens Complaint Board is among three suspects charged in the shooting death of a cab driver. Authorities identified [redacted], 16, after formally charging him as an adult with murder and robbery."[69]

Other ghosts of arrests past started haunting me. I remember receiving calls from City Legal every few weeks, telling me of yet another complaint about an arrest or traffic stop I made.

A local gun shop owner complained I was "rude" after I pulled him over. A female police officer who was at the scene when a pregnant female pulled a gun on me claimed I used excessive force during the encounter. I feel this incident in particular needs further explanation.

While it's true that I did push the woman's head into a wall, it was after she disobeyed my orders to show me her hands and instead began pulling a gun out of her purse. It was not obvious to me that she was pregnant. But the complaints that surfaced failed to take into account what happened on my end.

Every story took on the same theme: this violent officer who just killed an unarmed Black man also was rough with other suspects for no good reason. I sank deeper into a feeling of hopelessness as I realized I had no platform to defend myself or tell my side.

Mayor Hudnut was walking a political tightrope. Rev. Wayne T. Harris met with him and Mary Booker at Harris' church. The Reverend said he wanted Hudnut to feel Barnett's mother's pain. "I wanted him to hear the frustration of a mother's voice, to look in a mother's eyes," he said.[70]

In that meeting, Booker explained that she was incensed by my radio traffic immediately following the shooting. "He said, 'Send the paramedics for this clown.' He shouldn't have said that. That was a human life."[71] Hudnut replied in my defense that I was probably just "angry" because I had been chasing her son for nearly an hour. He stated, "I am unflinching and steadfast in my support of the law enforcement of this community… On the other hand, I'm also trying to say to the minority community and those who are aggravated by this most recent situation that we hear you—we are trying our best to not only understand your concerns, but to have an internal process of review of our procedures to see if there are areas where we can improve."[72]

Next came the Concerned Clergy's meeting with the prosecutor. Reporters asked Goldsmith whether the clergy wanted to meet with him as prosecutor or the next mayor of Indianapolis. "They addressed me as prosecutor, but it's clear the concerns they have are broader than just the prosecutor's office. Whether they want my support for those changes as prosecutor or potentially as mayor, I don't know," Goldsmith responded."[73]

In the end, he refused to step aside and seek a special prosecutor to investigate the incident.

The city continued to evaluate its review process of police action shootings. "Indianapolis Police officials will alter the way they investigate police shootings, and they have asked federal authorities to decide whether they should change the way they train recruits. In a news conference, Mayor Hudnut and Chief Annee announced:

- IPD's firearms review board, which traditionally has the first word on whether a police action shooting is justified, now must wait for a Marion County grand jury review.
- A newly formed investigative team will include other agencies, such as the Marion County Prosecutor's office, and end the practice of police investigating police.
- At the Mayor's request, the U.S. Department of Justice investigators will evaluate IPD's training procedures—the third such evaluation in a decade.

The Concerned Clergy responded with their displeasure. Michael Gradison, executive director of the Indiana Civil Liberties Union, was skeptical as well. The proposed changes still didn't address the actual firearms use policies. He responded, "It's still all part of the same team. It's still the government side."[74]

On October 16, 1990, *The Star* referred to the FBI investigation into whether the use of deadly force was criminal. The article read, "An Indianapolis policeman was justified in killing unarmed robbery suspect Leonard R. Barnett Jr., U.S. Attorney Deborah J. Daniels said Monday. Daniels, in announcing the decision of the Justice Department's civil rights division in Washington, said she reached the same conclusion after reviewing the local FBI investigation into the July 9 shooting. The Department of Justice has found no criminal civil rights violation on the part of Officer Haslar, given the information the officer possessed, and observations he was capable of making, in the moment in which he confronted Mr. Barnett."[75]

Had the investigation's findings been different, I would have been charged with federal criminal civil rights violations and potentially sent to prison.

Mary Booker said, "I figured it would turn out like that."[76]

Rev. Hannah of the Concerned Clergy said, "It bothers us in as much as we know that there are too many shootings of Black males."[77]

ACLU lawyer Richard Waples went on record, saying he would know later that week whether the family would proceed with a wrongful death lawsuit. Two days later on October 18, *The Star* read, "The mother of slain robbery suspect Leonard R. Barnett Jr., on Thursday accused an Indianapolis policeman of 'cold-blooded murder,' and sought her revenge in U.S. District Court. In a wrongful death lawsuit against Patrolman Scott L. Haslar, Mary Jo Booker said Haslar violated the civil rights of her unarmed son by using unnecessary deadly force on July 9."[78]

I still had to testify before the grand jury. Though I had been cleared by the Department of Justice (DOJ), I was still facing the possibility of indictment. The mayor's office commented, "We're hopeful that this [grand jury hearing] will begin soon and that the question of criminal intent or involvement will be duly answered by a civilian board—the grand jury—which we believe to be the best place to hear fatal shooting cases like this."[79]

The hearing was scheduled for December. I remember getting the notification letter delivered in the mail a few months prior, ordering me to show up on the specified date and time to testify. In the letter, as required by the state, the notification listed the most serious charge of which you could be indicted. In my case, it was murder.

I can still remember sitting in that chair waiting to testify before the jury, my legs bouncing, just like in that police car after the shooting. Sitting there, one thought haunted me—at the conclusion of my testimony, would I need to start preparing for a future murder trial, facing potential prison time? It was utterly terrifying.

I went in and testified with visceral emotion before the jury, trying to explain exactly what happened, from my recollection on July 9. After I finished and left the prosecutor's office, I felt some relief. I thought it went as well as it could. Any jury presents the accused with a feeling of total uncertainty. When a group of citizens as a collective unit is sitting in judgement of your actions, regardless of how well you feel your side presented, there's still the potential for the group to go high and right and come up with a conclusion that renders you the bad guy. I knew I had a 50/50 chance here.

On December 12, *The Star* reported, "Indianapolis policeman Scott L. Haslar was clearly justified in fatally shooting robbery suspect Leonard R. Barnett because he feared for his life, a Marion County special grand jury found Tuesday. The jury was "extremely critical," however, of the actions of other law enforcement officials involved in the high-speed chase with the 25-year-old man on July 9. "We are left with the unsettling conclusion that this is a shooting that didn't have to happen, but that Haslar acted within the law in firing his gun, said Marion County Prosecutor Stephen Goldsmith."[80]

The article reported criticisms regarding the lack of interagency cooperation and communication as well as of police procedures and tactics: Why didn't the officers on the initial stop order Barnett out of the car? Why didn't they take his keys? Where was supervisorial control of the pursuit incident?

Rev. Harris commented on the jury's ruling. "You can't legislate judgment. A bad call is just a bad call... Any shooting can be ruled justified if a police officer says he or she was in reasonable fear of danger. The law should more narrowly define what can be considered reasonable fear," he said."[81]

From my point of view, what Rev. Harris is suggesting is a slippery slope. It's nearly impossible to legislate the subjective nature of fear. There are just too many variables. The only recognized legal test is whether an officer was "objectively reasonable" in his actions or not pursuant to the Supreme Court case of Graham v. Connor. I was initially permitted to go back to street duty with the newly formed Special Operations and Response (SOAR) team. It was comprised of only SWAT officers, and we were assigned to patrol high-crime areas of the city when we weren't serving high-risk warrants for homicide, robbery, or narcotics branches.

Some were concerned, my parents included, that I might hesitate to defend myself on the street if my life was threatened again. Admittedly, I was, too.

One night during that first month back on the street, we were directed to patrol a dicey near-eastside neighborhood, or "the swamp," as it was referred to by officers. I was flagged down by a young Black male. He was very upset, and rightfully so, as he described how he had just been threatened by an older white male in a van as he walked across the parking lot to enter Snug Harbor, a local bar with a mostly white clientele. He said the man pointed a gun at him and said, "This bar isn't a bar for your kind." Soon after, he flagged me down. I alerted officers in the area and began looking for the vehicle. I spotted it nearby and stopped it.

The suspect was just as the victim described. As I positioned myself next to the driver's door of the van, holding my chemical spray in my left hand, I asked him for his license and registration. Instead, the intoxicated and belligerent man reached for a gun between the seats. I immediately sprayed him in the face and ran to the rear of the van for cover as I drew my weapon. There, I looked through the rear window. I saw he was aiming a pistol at where I had been standing.

I aligned my sights directly on the back of his head. In that split second before pulling the trigger, he dropped the weapon and started rubbing his eyes from the spray, just as a SWAT sergeant arrived to assist. He immediately pulled the guy out of the van and handcuffed him.

The next day, Wayne Voida wrote me up for a commendation, which is an inter-departmental recognition for going above and beyond on the job. Voida thought my ability to use discretion and restraint in the situation should be acknowledged. The higher-ups didn't think so. One of them said, "How would it look if it was revealed that you didn't shoot an armed white guy during a traffic stop, but shot and killed an unarmed Black man during another?"

They reassigned me to desk duty again. Of course, they acknowledged the circumstances were different between the two situations, but they knew how it would look to the public. At that point, it was all about the politics of perception.

Did I hesitate to use my weapon in this situation because of the Barnett shooting, or is the choice to use deadly force just that fast and fluid? If the driver of the van had not dropped his weapon almost immediately as his hands came up, I feel certain I would have shot him. Every situation is different and must be objectively analyzed as such—absent the politics of race and perception involved.

I was off the street; I was still on SWAT, responding to call-ups and activations of the team. But the supervisors would not assign me to the front of the team (the first officers to enter) on high-risk felony warrant services, keeping me at the tail end of the stack. On full call-ups, such as barricaded subjects or hostage situations, I was assigned to perimeter containment or command and control aide positions.

SWAT's quintessential function is to rescue hostages. I believe they worried about me hesitating in a life or death situation. An innocent civilian could die. We also knew each other pretty well. Specialized tactical team members tend to become like brothers. They didn't think I could handle another potentially controversial shooting. I believe they acted in the team's best interest, mine as well. To them, it was for my own good and not politically motivated at all.

I continued to report to work every day, but I was assigned to jobs I wouldn't have chosen myself. The options my superiors presented me with were low-profile and low-risk positions. I know they were trying to diminish the chance of me using deadly force again, but I joined the police department to be a street cop—not a detective or an administrator.

I tried the Family Abuse Unit, which was responsible for investigating child abuse. Those were probably the hardest, most emotionally draining assignments I ever experienced. I talked with kids that had been sexually molested and/or beaten. I watched as photos were taken of the welts and bruises dealt by their caretakers with belt buckles and other instruments. It was gut-wrenching to see those kids day after day and witness the aftermath of their suffering.

I will never forget a sweet little red-headed Pippi-Longstocking-looking six-year-old girl whose case I was assigned.

I had the cigarette burns up and down her arms, legs, and back photographed. I was no forensic pathologist, but even I could immediately tell this had been going on for quite some time. Some wounds were old and healed, and some were fresh. I can't remember the details of the story she told me about how she'd gotten them, but it didn't add up.

After I gently asked her if she was telling the truth, she admitted her father had told her to tell that story to anyone who asked, including teachers, neighbors, and especially the police. He scared her into thinking she would be taken away from him if she didn't lie.

During the interview with the father, he gave me the same lies he'd fed the girl. In the middle of the interview, I remember him asking, "Can we take a break? I need a cigarette." It was everything I could do not to come across the table at this guy. When talking to these abusers, you have to become friends with them in order to get them to spill. "If that were my kid, I wouldn't stand for that either," or "Yeah, I can see how you became aroused seeing her dressed in those pajamas." At times, you walk that line of becoming a monster in order to catch one.

As we neared the end of 1990, *The Star* ran an article announcing their picks for the top ten news stories of the year in Indiana. Number one was the death of Ryan White, the young boy who valiantly fought the deadly autoimmune deficiency syndrome. His funeral brought visits to the Indianapolis area from public figures such as Michael Jackson, Elton John, and Barbara Bush.

My shooting and the ensuing media war made the number two spot.

The two friends I mentioned earlier, alcohol and isolation, were now my daily companions. I was a household name in Indianapolis, and I was incredibly uncomfortable in that knowledge.

CHAPTER 5

CONTROVERSIAL COP

In came 1991—a new year and nothing to celebrate. We were just a few months in when a new embroilment called my name back into the spotlight, rekindling the media war between IPD, the mayor's office, and the Concerned Clergy. And it was an event just as provocative as the shooting.

On March 7, I was awarded IPD's Medal of Valor by a peer committee in a public ceremony.

At this point in the story, as I try to describe what was happening for me as I received the medal and then weathered the backlash, it occurs to me I've repeated the following phrase over and over again: "I don't remember much of that event." It's an unfortunate but true statement that I find just as frustrating as perhaps the reader does. I'm reexamining these memories and experiences 30 years later after having repressed and medicated them away for so long. There was no journaling. No therapy appointments. Save for Tammy, I didn't confide in anyone throughout those years, and even she acknowledges that eventually, I also stopped confiding in her.

The details in my mind of that award ceremony are fuzzy. I didn't know I was receiving the medal. All I was told by my superiors was that I had to be there that afternoon. I was reluctant to go as I hated attending public events, but I had no choice. When they announced my name from the stage, I was shocked. I couldn't imagine, after everything that unfolded after the shooting, that I was receiving an award related to it. My entire body shook with anxiety as I stood and walked up to the stage, flashes from the media's cameras lighting my path. Somewhere inside, I think I felt pride that I was being acknowledged for doing what I felt I had to do on that July night, yet my overwhelming feelings were tension and discomfort. I could sense the audience, comprised of department personnel and media, felt it as well. I didn't know what to do.

As the crowd broke into an apprehensive applause, something completely unexpected happened. Sgt. Stephen Fitzpatrick (or Fitz, as I call him) said he and a fellow officer sitting next to him had an inkling that I would be receiving an award that day, so prior to the ceremony, they came up with a plan. "I remember us talking about how much shit you'd been going through," Fitz said. When my name was announced, they stood up in unison, starting a standing ovation that slowly spread throughout the audience. Every person was now on their feet applauding me as the medal was placed around my neck. It was a surreal moment. Fitz eventually became, and still is, one of my closest friends. He was at my side through several of the personal and professional tragedies that unfolded in the ensuing years.

The next day, the front page of *The Star*'s City/State section ran a photo of me wearing the medal with Officer Theresa Hedge congratulating me. The story read, "The Indianapolis Police Department gave its highest honor to its most controversial cop, applauding Patrolman Scott Haslar for his actions in the fatal shooting of robbery suspect Leonard Barnett."[82] (The Medal of Valor is actually the department's second-highest honor, its first being the Medal of Honor.)

Controversial Cop—the moniker bestowed upon me by the media after receiving the award. And it stuck. It would be used again and again over the next few years, along with the phrase, "Shoot a Black, get a plaque."

My father penned a letter to the editor dated that same day. He was not happy about the media's portrayal of me. He wrote, "In reference to your article of March 8, 1991 in Section B-1. Your lead title is 'Controversial cop gets medal.' Scott Haslar is not a controversial cop, in fact he is an excellent policeman with a fine proven track record. Perhaps a better title would have been 'Policeman involved in controversial shooting gets medal.'" Dad's letter-writing career was in full swing by now.

The mayor's office and Chief Annee initially made statements in the article showing support for the award. "While no person takes pleasure in the death of another, we do intend to honor those who make critical decisions on our behalf," a mayoral staff representative replied.[83] Of the award committee's recommendation, he said, "If I had any qualms about it, he wouldn't have received the award. I don't think you can take away from the difficulty of the situation that Officer Haslar faced just because of the controversy.

He has been exonerated by every agency that has investigated it. It certainly isn't meant as an affront to the Barnett family or the Black community."[84]

The ACLU's Michael Gradison said he was, "… stunned by it. It seems to me that other police officers have done nobler things."[85] Others were plain outraged. "I'm appalled by the award," said Steven L. Barnett (not related to Leonard Barnett), a Democrat and the only Black mayoral candidate. He continued, "Not because it was a Black man—I can't see awarding anyone for the taking of a life."[86] Muhammad Siddeeq called the award, "… a callous insensitivity to African American life in Indianapolis… Why a Medal of Valor which seems to approve and endorse the killing of African American males?"[87] A.D. Pinckney, Jr., president of the NAACP, weighed in by saying, "The NAACP feels that this will be interpreted by bigots and those who promote racial hatred that they have the support of the police department."[88]

Mayor Hudnut, who was out of town during the awards process and not involved with the decision, according to a press release from his office, now appeared to be backtracking on his original show of support for me and the department. His statement read, "The award was not given for killing a young Black man in our community, I'm sure of that. But I'm also acutely aware that this event is being perceived as an affront and an insult to Mr. Barnett's family and to the African American community in Indianapolis. I feel very badly about this and about the insensitivity involved. I have discussed this with the chief of police and informed him of my displeasure. He has accepted responsibility and assured me that it will not happen again."[89] After a statement like that from the mayor, it wasn't hard to predict that Chief Annee would soon be changing his tune regarding the award.

After a few months of relative quiet at the City-County building, the Medal of Valor rekindled protests.

"Rescind Award or Resign Job,"[90] read a sign at the demonstration, where at least 100 people gathered again in front of police headquarters.

Here we go again, I thought. I began bracing for the next round of both public support and lashings—the manic/depressive cycle—the juxtaposition of two passionately opposing opinions I'd become so familiar with.

"How can you give a man a medal for killing an unarmed man, a man that was injured. I just can't understand that,"[91] Mary Booker said at the protest. Muhammad Siddeeq screamed to the crowd, "We're not here to divide the city, but we are here to let Indianapolis know that such a callous and insensitive act cannot go unchallenged."[92]

Not surprisingly, the once unwavering support from the chief began to dissolve in the tidal wave of headlines and rally cries. In a follow-up article the day after the protest, Chief Annee apologized for the award. "Indianapolis Police Chief Paul Annee's apology for a controversy over a departmental award apparently is not the last word that he hoped he would hear. The unprecedented—and, some said, uncharacteristic—written statement issued Wednesday did not satisfy all critics of the Medal of Valor given to Patrolman Scott Haslar. And the beleaguered chief's reversal opened him up to fresh criticism from his department's police union."[93] Although he acknowledged I had faced an extremely difficult situation that night, Annee stated, "Something like this will not happen again as long as I am chief."[94]

Dad took to his typewriter once again to fire off a letter to Mayor Hudnut, which he copied to Chief Annee. Interesting excerpts include:

> Your comments in the March 13 Indianapolis Star are most disturbing to me, both as a citizen of the City and the father of Scott Haslar. It appears your comments are not for the City or even the overall Black Community, but aimed to appease a group of Black Ministers and their limited followers.
>
> I would like to remind you that each of the agencies found Scott 100% justified in his actions including the Marion County Grand Jury that consisted of both white and Black jurors.
>
> It is starting to appear, that through your lack of support and the overzealous news media that Leonard Barnett should have received an award for being a robber and holding a gun at someone's head!
>
> In my opinion it's time someone at your level strongly support the police and Scott and quit trying to appease Wayne T. Harris, Mike Gradison, Muhammad Siddeeq and their followers.
>
> I cannot speak for Scott, but if it were me, I would drop the award in the middle of your desk, and let you present it to Wayne T. Harris for his great role in helping Black Youths choose the right path in life!!

A week later, Mayor Hudnut sent a personal letter back to Dad. The envelope it arrived in, preserved all these years by my mom, is considerably thick. It addressed each point in the letter and included supporting documents. Here are a few excerpts:

> Thank you for taking the time to write. Please find enclosed a copy of the statement I issued after the uproar in the community was heard about the award. You may not agree with it, Sir, but I am trying my best to exercise a level head and hand in this matter. I have no quarrel with many points you made in your letter. Your son was in a life-threatening situation and with the information he had, acted professionally and properly and has been upheld by the review agencies. I also sympathize with him and your family for the pain and grief he has gone through since last July 9. I hope you can sympathize with my efforts to keep this community from blowing apart. People like myself and the chief are walking a very taut tightrope, and it is very difficult to hold everyone together, much less make anyone on either side happy.
>
> I do take exception, however, to your comments about my not supporting the Police Department. I feel that my refusal to yield to considerable pressure to fire the Chief and/or rescind the award to your son represents strong backing of the IPD.

Hudnut went on to point out the increase in wages and benefits for police officers he achieved during his tenure in the office. He enclosed a copy of a budget speech he delivered before the City-County Council in 1990. He also included a copy of a short letter addressed to the mayor from the FOP, thanking him for his words of support in August of 1990, shortly after the shooting. Hudnut signed his letter to Dad:

> With kindest personal regards to you, I am
>
> Cordially yours,
>
> William H. Hudnut, III

After the mayor issued his public statement of displeasure with the award, I confess I was angry with him. Even though we didn't discuss the ordeal much as a family, my feelings were similar to Dad's. Looking back now, I realize that Hudnut was in a difficult position, but he took the time to personally respond to my dad, which he didn't have to do. Though it wasn't the unconditional show of support we were hungry for at the time, it seems that Hudnut, in his own way, was trying to build a bridge between the two sides.

But hindsight is 20/20. My reaction at the time? Disappointment. Confusion. Anxiety. Anger. The usual cocktail of negative feelings I held at bay by winding them tightly within myself.

Letters to the editor saw a resurgence, and as the current political and racial divide dictated, some were in staunch support of the medal, while others were in strong opposition. An IPD police lieutenant who sat on the awards committee weighed in. In a front-page article in *The Star*, Lt. Frank Jameson, III, stated, "Patrolman Scott L. Haslar, who is white, did not receive the award for shooting a Black person." He continued, "I'm Black and I'm not offended."[95] He said my actions fit the award criteria for the Medal of Valor, which state: "It shall be awarded to any officer for an act that exemplifies heroism and valor. The officer shall demonstrate courageous behavior upon being confronted with a potentially dangerous adversary."[96]

The citizens offered their opinions, both in defense and condemnation of the award.

Some of the criticisms: "While I wholeheartedly agree that giving the police department's highest award to Patrolman Scott Haslar, who shot Leonard Barnett, was an act of callous insensitivity, a major message may have been missed,"[97] wrote Gerald Cunningham. He continued, "Apparently that message is that an Indianapolis police officer will be protected, supported, even awarded for using lethal force against unarmed 'suspects' even under the most questionable and controversial circumstances."[98]

Henry Whitehead wrote, "The Indianapolis Police Department has thumbed its nose at African Americans, letting them know their opinions and feelings carry no weight in dealing with questionable practices by individual officers. In the Barnett shooting, no weapon was found, the suspect had been severely wounded prior to being shot and killed, and the threat to Haslar was his own fear. That was the basis for his excessive force. Does that merit an award for valor?"[99]

Some of the support: Harold Davidson wrote, "I'm tired of hearing militant Black ministers claiming racism and murder whenever a white policeman kills a criminal. The skin color of the cop or crook makes absolutely no difference."[100]

Benjamin Schreiber said the Concerned Clergy was inciting racism with their reactions. "I write this neither in support nor condemnation of the award given to Scott Haslar, but to question the validity of some Indianapolis Black ministers' statements. I disagree that this was a racial incident. No matter what race, people who perpetrate a chase like that would be shot given the same circumstances. It is time that influential community leaders stop using incidents like this to incite racism. I am certain that if a white suspect were shot, we would not hear from the Black ministers."[101]

Days before I received the medal, a police/community conflict was exploding on a national level. The Rodney King incident occurred on March 3, 1991. King was a Black motorist who led police on a high-speed chase in Los Angeles that culminated in a violent apprehension caught on videotape by an eyewitness. The incident dominated local and national media coverage.

Rodney King became a springboard for comparisons to my case. Indianapolis community members, along with the Concerned Clergy, brought my name back into the media and also revisited claims of a racist IPD. Another protest ensued, as well as more letters to the editor.

A letter in *The Star* from Ernest J. Newborn, Sr. of Indianapolis read, "Duty of police: 'To protect and serve.' This is the policeman's motto. It evokes a high sense of duty and ethics. The behavior of Los Angeles police officers… seems an egregious abridgement of both duty and ethics. I have difficulty understanding why the Indianapolis Police Department selected for special honor a policeman who shot an unarmed man after a car chase. It is noted that the victims in both tragic incidents are Black males. As the father of a young Black male, I worry about the possibility that my son could become a victim of police brutality…"[102]

As for the Concerned Clergy, they went back to the streets. One citizen thought this was a calculated spectacle fueled by the desire for publicity rather than peace. There was an opportunity for national coverage in Indianapolis at the time. The 1991 Final Four's end to "March Madness" was set to play out at the Hoosier Dome, making for an ideal platform.

Ed Hutchinson wrote, "After saturation media coverage of local anti-police groups such as the Indiana Civil Liberties Union, the National Association for the Advancement of Colored People, the Urban League, etc., and after non-stop coverage of the Los Angeles police beating Rodney King, the Concerned Clergy of Indianapolis decided it was time to act.

With camera crews from around the nation in town to cover the Final Four tournament, the Concerned Clergy called a protest rally to show the country the outrage that exists in Indianapolis over recent police action shootings. Fifty persons showed up... Every local and federal agency with the power to review the police shootings in question have done so and found no wrongs committed..."[103] The remainder of that spring, there were sporadic articles, but the onslaught slowed considerably.

Then in July of 1991, *The Star* featured a front-page article in their Focus section titled, "A Year After the Shooting..."[104]

Star reporter Kevin Morgan wrote, "Who knows how fast Leonard Barnett was going through the morning darkness, west on 10th Street, under the interstate, toward the little zigzag at College Ave. Probably 100 mph, according to the army of police that chased him, off and on, from Castleton. The airbag was probably all that kept Barnett alive when the borrowed Camaro bounced off a house at 10th and College. Pathologists believe the first of five shots from Patrolman Scott Haslar's semi-automatic might have been enough to kill Barnett. The 25-year-old-man didn't die for another hour. If only Barnett could have seen the impact of his life."[105] Morgan interviewed Mary Booker, Rev. Wayne T. Harris, Rev. William Hannah, and Chief Annee. He wrote, "The death of Leonard Barnett had started each of the four on a personal odyssey—measured not in distance or speed but in the causes they found and the lessons they learned."[106]

Mary Booker said she wasn't surprised that the police failed to locate the weapon her son reportedly brandished. Morgan wrote, "Her son didn't like guns... Her son wasn't a holdup man."[107]

Rev. Hannah, who, according to the article, once marched with the Rev. Dr. Martin Luther King Jr., said his mayoral appointment to the Citizens Complaint Review Board last summer and the Barnett shooting once again ignited his anger and activism. Hannah stated he quickly became fed up as review boards cleared me and the Citizens' Complaint Board was denied review privileges of the shooting. Rev. Hannah's statements suggested the Midwestern metropolis of Indianapolis just didn't get it. He said, "I think Indianapolis has grown so fast in the last few years that I don't think that the ruralness has been able to keep up with the urban-ness. We still have a lot of people who still remember the Ku Klux Klan here. I think that we've got a lot of problems, but I think that they can be worked out. I'm just hoping and praying that reasonable people are going to be able to reason out some way that we can coexist without all the tension."[108]

In the end, Hannah was offering a hope for collective mutual understanding and healing—a hope I still hold to 32 years later.

It seemed a year later, Rev. Wayne T. Harris was able to find a more neutral perspective on the ordeal. He said, "It would be wrong—it would be irresponsible as a so-called community leader for me to keep as if we were still holding guns at each other with no point of coming together, when in fact this administration has started to melt like ice... You would have to have seen the cold nature that we perceived, the cold nature of Paul Annee in the past. For him to make the statement that he did, to do anything like an apology—I saw it as a warming of the Indianapolis Police Department. What else could we have done but accept his apology?"[109]

Chief Annee said, "I had nothing to do with the shooting. You know, I'm the police chief, and I'm responsible for what happens in the organization, and I understand that. I accept that responsibility. But the medal situation was different. I think I was more vulnerable—if that's the right word—to criticism. And maybe more justifiably so. This whole concept of being insensitive, this whole concept of not considering others' feelings in some of these very sensitive and emotional situations... yeah, I think that would be a fair statement to make... I think Rev. Harris will tell you that for the first time, he saw me and the department make some acknowledgement that we can make mistakes from time to time and we aren't perfect. We never thought for a minute that we were. We make a lot of mistakes every day."[110]

He contemplated whether the next administration would keep him on as chief, or if he would want to continue in the role. He noted that cumulative stress is chronic. He said, "I don't think you can reach your potential as a police chief until you've experienced the kind of things we've experienced over the past few years. It will either run you off or it will sensitize you, one or the other. But they're not easy; they're not easy personally. They're tough on my family. I don't know that it's affected my health, but I don't know of any more stress-packed position in local government today."[111]

I do not remember Morgan contacting me or my lawyer for a statement.

The remainder of that year, I continued to show up for work. Preparation for the civil suit began, along with depositions—a series of interrogations that lasted the better part of a week.

The plaintiff's attorney, Richard Waples, initially came off in the depositions as some sort of neutral, unbiased factfinder who was seeking the "truth" of the situation. However, I quickly learned not to freely expound on any question when a, "Yes, sir," or "No, Sir," would suffice. As I now know from first-hand experience, the plaintiff's counsel's goals are to lock you into statements that could be used against you in the trial.

I also was ordered to answer interrogatories, or a series of questions asked in preparation for a federal civil case, wherein both parties—plaintiff and defense—are entitled to obtain personal information about the other. The majority of the questions from what I recall were tied to my net worth. I had to provide several years' worth of W-2's and answer questions about my property and investments.

What became quite clear to me was that the plaintiff wasn't just going after monetary damages from the City of Indianapolis.

They were gunning for my personal bank account as well. My defense team informed me that the potential settlement could come from combined compensatory damages for loss and suffering, and punitive damages awarded to punish the officer for his/her actions. Compensatory damages were "customarily," as my team said, paid by the department for "within the scope" of on-duty actions. Punitive damages, on the other hand, might come out of your own pocket.

Damages sought by the Barnett estate were in the millions. My annual salary when I began my career was $14,401. I was young and owned nothing outright. Based on my net worth, it would take me several lifetimes of garnished wages to pay back a settlement in the proposed sums. The gravity of what I was facing was not only psychological and spiritual, but now, financial.

CHAPTER 6

FEDERAL TRIALS AND TRIBULATIONS

The year 1990 brought the shooting. 1991 brought the Medal of Valor. 1992 should have brought nothing but joy, because our daughter was born. But if I had in fact made some sort of divine contract with Leonard Barnett, it had not been fully executed yet. The journey our souls walked together, though mine was of earth and his was not, continued.

For Indianapolis, 1992 began with a new leader at the helm. Former prosecutor Stephen Goldsmith, who found himself in the center of the media war in 1990 when he refused to disqualify himself by appointing a special prosecutor, was elected the 46th mayor by a clear majority and took office January 1, 1992. Indianapolis also had a new chief of police, James D. Toler, who succeeded Annee. Chief Toler was the first Black man to hold the position.

Despite the fact I was preparing for my first federal trial, there was, in fact, finally something to celebrate in my life. Tammy was expecting. So, I also was preparing for my first foray into parenthood. I felt the normal anxieties that come with being a new father.

Could I do this? Could I get it right? This particular nervousness was exciting, and it was a welcome relief from the anxiety of the public train wreck I'd been dealing with. Our daughter Madi was born just a month before the trial. As I watched her birth in the labor room, for a moment, all of the pressure and tension of the last two years paused.

As Tammy and I continued to navigate parenthood, full-time jobs, and the stress of the upcoming legal proceedings, I continued meeting with my legal team on a regular basis. The trial was set for the fall. The lawsuit alleged I had violated Barnett's rights under the Fourth Amendment to the Constitution, which specifically prohibits unreasonable seizures. Killing someone in the line of duty is viewed as the ultimate seizure.

I also was being sued under the Fourteenth Amendment and its due process clause. In other words, the plaintiff claimed I had deprived Barnett of life, liberty, and the pursuit of happiness by preventing him from getting a fair day in court to answer for his alleged robbery.

The weekend before the trial began, I felt as if the newspapers were priming the public for a collective outrage, so I braced myself for the week ahead. Saturday, Kevin O'Neal of *The Indianapolis News* wrote, "The distance from 10th Street and College Avenue to the U.S. Courthouse is one mile. It's taken two years for the Leonard Barnett case to travel that distance." William Crawford, Democrat state representative from Indianapolis, added, "If the jury exonerates the police, I think there will be a reaction, although it won't be as violent as the Rodney King reaction."[112]

Waples made a statement in the media, saying he thought he'd spend a good deal of time with the jury selection process. He said he wanted to make sure the jurors selected weren't prejudiced against Black people, or people accused of crimes.[113] On the other side, the article reported, my team wanted to make sure that jurors selected weren't biased against police officers nor thought they routinely used excessive force.

The trial began. I recall toting Madi to the courthouse nearly every day in her little pumpkin seat. Some of her attendance was out of necessity because Tammy was breastfeeding. But the primary reason was by design, commissioned by my defense team. My lawyers thought if I was seen carrying my baby into the courtroom, I might just appear human after all.

Day I. On Monday, September 14, jury selection began in the morning. I sat anxiously listening as the lawyers questioned potential jurors, my legs bouncing underneath the defense table. I was dressed in my new, impeccably pressed dark blue police uniform, which my team told me to wear. Every so often, Kautzman, the lead counsel, would whisper to me, "What do you think of this one," or, "Should we keep or dismiss this one?" I answered as best I could, having no frame of reference of what it meant to decide who should sit in judgement of me.

More than 40 people were called as potential jurors. A six-member jury was finally selected. Opening statements began later that afternoon.

I walked back into the courtroom flanked by my team and took my seat at the defense table. The plaintiff's team entered after and took their posts on the other side of the room. It was all very serious and somber. After everyone was seated, we waited in what seemed like hours of quiet tension. Finally, the bailiff bellowed, "All rise!" As I stood, I gaped at the judge as if seeing him for the first time. He now appeared a much larger man—an intense and imposing figure, donning his long black robe and walking with purpose up to his bench. He sat, and we followed. He shuffled a few papers, took a second to collect himself, then looked over at the bailiff and ordered, "Bring in the jury."

My stomach dropped.

The seven members of the jury shuffled into the room (six jurors plus one alternate), single file, and took their seats in the jury box.

The plaintiff's counsel got first shot. Waples opened with a bang, clearly illustrating his theory: I was dishonest in my description of the shooting. He said, "This was an unjustified police shooting. I think the evidence will show that Haslar didn't have the right to shoot him. The officer's version is directly contradicted by witnesses and physical evidence."[114] "When police officers violate the law and then lie to cover it up, we have all lost something," he said.[115]

Barnett had been severely injured in the crash and would not have been able to move, he said. "So, Haslar is lying when he claims he shot Barnett after the suspect ran to his car and rummaged inside, as if looking for something."[116] In his condition, Waples said Barnett would have only been able to possibly hobble, especially not run as I claimed. "Officer Haslar created a terrible scheme which had Leonard running like a track star, despite a badly broken leg."[117]

He concluded with saying that my statement contained at least four lies, and he intended to lay each one out for the jury.[118]

As I sat listening to Waples, I was stunned by the picture he painted of me. I didn't recognize the man he described. He was portraying me as an angry, hateful officer who was treating Barnett with disgust and disdain that night. He reenacted the confrontation in a highly theatrical manner, repeating the commands I gave to Barnett that night with vitriol and aggression in his voice. He screamed at the jury, as he said I had done that night, "Get on the fucking ground!" He completely reframed the shooting as a story of an angry cop who killed a man, then lied about the circumstances.

Thomas Carusillo, a member of my defense team, opened with, "There is another side to this story."[119] In comparing apparent inconsistencies, Carusillo advised the jury, "There are no lies. Are there disparities among witnesses? You bet there are. People don't all necessarily see the same thing the same way."[120] He explained that police officers, by the nature of the position they hold, are permitted to use force, even deadly force, if it is reasonable, and he laid out the events of that night to illustrate that my use of deadly force was, in fact, reasonable. When he returned to the crashed Camaro after I'd ordered him to the ground, Barnett gave me two choices, Carusillo emphatically told to the jury, "Do I shoot, or do I get shot?"[121]

After opening statements, the first witness was called. Donald Smith stated that he was driving north on College Avenue at the time of my shooting. "Ahead of him, from 75 to 100 feet away, he testified, he saw Haslar get out of his car and run toward Barnett, who was standing in the street. Haslar ran circling the suspect until he was north of Barnett, Smith said. Barnett turned to his left and that's when the shots started."[122]

Kautzman's plan was to discredit Smith's testimony by introducing his previous criminal history. Waples objected, but Judge McKinney allowed it.[123]

During a spontaneous cross examination, Kautzman turned his attention to whether Smith was a reliable eyewitness to the shooting, given his description of watching it from a "crouched position" in his driver's seat. He asked Smith, "Can you show me?" Smith slid down in the witness chair. Kautzman confirmed, "Like that?" Smith said yes. But he was down so far in his seat that he couldn't see the jury, and the jury couldn't see him. Kautzman proved that much of his testimony was based on assumption and speculation.

Another eyewitness who testified was in a vehicle directly behind Smith. He seemed to still be traumatized from witnessing the shooting a few years prior. During his testimony, he said that after he heard the first of the shots, he quickly turned around, and in his words, "I got the hell outta Dodge!" In the days that followed the shooting, he said he knew he had to get out of the big city. He moved back home to Kentucky after the incident.

Day II. Waples continued to build on his theory that my account was fabricated. They called Jeff Mitchell, a young college student who said he saw the aftermath of the crash from his apartment window. He testified that he saw Barnett, "crouched down in the street, not really laying, not really standing." He said he saw me walk up to Barnett, then step away. Mitchell said he looked away when he heard the police car crash into the bus. He then heard five shots and when he turned back, he saw me but not Barnett. He testified he didn't tell police until two days later when the news accounts didn't match what he saw.[124]

Terry Young testified next, a paramedic who was on the scene that night. About Barnett's ankle, she said he might still have been able to walk, but she warned another paramedic, "Be careful with the ankle, because if not, we could take it off."[125]

The plaintiff's expert witness, orthopedist Dr. John E. Young, later testified, "I see no way that this injured ankle could bear weight and transfer weight from one foot to the other, which is required for walking or running." He went on to describe the injury in detail, concluding with, "In my professional opinion, he was not able to walk."[126] In cross examination, Kautzman asked him how Barnett managed to get out of the car and make it several feet away from the crashed vehicle. He said he had no explanation.

One of the first responding medics, Andrew Bowes, testified, "I have not seen anyone run or walk normally on an injury like that. I suppose he could have hopped or limped."[127] In Kautzman's cross examination, Bowes admitted that in his experience, "A disabled person can do anything if the adrenaline is pumping."[128]

Day III. I was slated to take the stand in my own defense on Wednesday. The anticipatory anxiety was overwhelming. *The Indianapolis News* reported that a blue line of officers was in attendance to support me. The article read, "12 officers sat down together, a solid line of support for their fellow officer."[129] I wish I could remember seeing my co-workers and feeling their support.

Unfortunately, I was so caught up in my own head and consumed with stress that it didn't register to me at the time.

After raising my right hand and answering the standard questions regarding name, rank, and place of employment, it was reported that I spent the next two hours and 37 minutes describing my decisions and actions on the night of the shooting. Reading that in a newspaper clipping all these years later took me aback.[130]

Two hours and 37 minutes to describe an incident which, after the investigators calculated the length of the encounter by timing the radio traffic, spanned just 43 seconds of time.

43 seconds.

Think about all the mundane decisions you make every day that take more time than 43 seconds. Then think about making a life-or-death decision within that time frame.

In my testimony that day, I said that based on the radio reports I heard from other officers and control operators, I believed Barnett was still armed and very dangerous when I confronted him at 10th and College. I stated that Barnett somehow got out of the vehicle. I started screaming, "Get on the fucking ground," but he would not comply. He abruptly came at me and, "… grabbed my shoulder and arm, as if he were trying to get my gun with both hands."[131]

I continued that I fended Barnett off by striking him with the palm heal of my left hand. I even demonstrated the technique with Kautzman in front of the jury. As I recall, this got a laugh from the courtroom as I hit him as hard as I possibly could, knocking him backward into a stumble. He prearranged this and told me to hit him just like I hit Barnett. I testified that at that moment, I thought

Barnett was going to go back to the vehicle. I screamed, "Don't go back to the car. Don't go back to the car!"[132]

Waples was brutal in his cross-examination. In response to him hammering me with the question of whether or not Barnett really did grab me, I finally answered in exasperation, "I don't know if he physically grabbed me. He was going for my arms."[133] I would have been looking directly at his face at that point. But in that moment on the stand, I didn't have the presence of mind, nor the time, to explain all of that. When crossed, I stated that I wasn't looking at his legs or feet, so I wasn't sure how he was able to move about. As was engrained in us at the academy, it's the hands that will kill you. I replied, "I was watching his hands and his face. I don't know if it was a hop, skip, or a jump. All I know is that he covered that distance. I was focused on his hands and his upper body." [134]

I continued my account. He made it back to the car and dove head-first into the driver's window. After rummaging through the vehicle for several seconds, he came back out. I believed he had grabbed the weapon used in the robbery and would soon use it against me. I said on the stand, "At that point, I knew it was him or me. He was coming out of the vehicle as I was shooting."[135] By the time I saw his empty hands, I had already fired five times, I said. "It's the most frightening thing I've ever been involved in."[136]

Muhammad Siddeeq was quoted after my day's testimony ended. "It appears there is not much truth in him. He's just a cold-blooded liar, as well as a killer." He continued, "If the verdict comes down in favor of the officer, it is going to confirm mistrust and make a bigger gulf between the community and the police." [137]

Day IV. One of the first responding IPD supervisors that night was Lt. Richard Proffitt. He testified that he didn't hear the shots fired as he approached the scene because of the responding sirens, but he did see Barnett lean into the car through the window, calling his moves, "very erratic."[138] He saw Barnett turn toward me and then stumble several feet toward the car, falling.[139]

Dr. Dean Hawley, the pathologist who performed Barnett's autopsy, testified that Barnett could have walked. "Was there any medical evidence that Leonard Barnett would have been unable to continue to function and ambulate due to the compound fracture?"[140] Kautzman asked Hawley. "For a limited period of time after sustaining these injuries, some mobility would have been possible,"[141] he answered. During cross-examination, however, Hawley was forced to admit that he was not an orthopedics-trained physician. Therefore, according to the plaintiff, he was not as qualified as their orthopedic surgeon.

Day V. After closing arguments on Friday, September 18, the case was turned over to the jury. Waples began his closing argument next to a large photo of Leonard Barnett, set in a chair at the plaintiff's table. He stood behind it as he addressed the jury, at times putting his hands on the photo, almost as if he was laying them on Barnett's shoulders. "So what's the truth about what happened at 10th and College, because that's what this case is about,"[142] Waples said. "He [Barnett] had just come through a violent collision. His foot was dangling off of his leg. He's staring down the barrel of a gun. What's he do? He had no reason to go back to that car."[143]

Waples then referenced Rebecca, a woman who lived in the house where the Camaro crashed. She testified that she thought she heard someone in a high-pitched voice yell, "No, no, don't!" Waples insinuated the voice came from Barnett. He concluded, "He started to turn like this, and Officer Haslar shot him down in the street. He fell backward into the drainage ditch and died."

His words sent my thoughts reeling: *No, he's got it wrong! It was the high-pitched voice of a terrified cop screeching like a pubescent teen, "No, no, don't go back to the car!"* I don't recall Barnett ever uttering one word. Would the jury make that connection, or would they believe it was Barnett's voice?

Looking at these old newspaper clippings and photographs brings back all the thoughts that were racing through my mind and the bodily reactions that rocked my tenuous foundation. I can still feel the waves of judgment crashing over me during closing arguments—all week long for that matter—along with the associated anxiety, fear, and admittedly, anger.

My thoughts: *Could they actually be buying this incredulous bullshit Waples is spinning?*

Looking back now, that young officer sitting in the defendant seat, thinking those thoughts, trying not to stand up and scream in outrage—he didn't have the advantage I have today of time, maturity, and life experience. Waples wasn't being paid to represent my truth. He was being paid to represent Barnett's truth. He was just doing his job.

Also, I can see that some of what Waples said was true, technically, but it was spun to paint me as the bad guy. Despite the indignation that overwhelmed me as I listened to him describe me, I could show no emotion. The jury was watching me like a hawk in the closing arguments, just as they had been every minute since opening statements. I hoped they couldn't see my legs bouncing underneath the table, or the sweat bleeding through my shirt like ink stains. Any slight show of emotion or anger might lead them to believe I was, as portrayed, that loose cannon just looking for someone to kill that morning.

I tried to calm myself with reason: *Stop bouncing. The jury has heard our testimony and seen evidence that contradicts Waples' allegations. John will clear this up in our closing argument.*

But which of the two truths presented will they decide to accept in their deliberation?

Carusillo began our closing argument. He conceded that witnesses on both sides placed both Barnett and me at differing locations and times, each seeing what they perceived. "The reason Leonard Barnett Junior was shot is because he went to that car and started going around in there. He appeared to be going for a gun."[144] Kautzman then took over and concluded with, "I believe in Scott Haslar and I believe in what he was trying to do for us out there that night, and I believe that you, too, believe that he acted as a reasonable police officer based on all the circumstances presented to him. You heard the evidence in this case. There are perspectives from everywhere. But you have the best perspective of all," he said as he motioned to me, "someone who has experienced it, saw it."[145]

The jury began deliberations around 3:15 p.m. My team and I went to a nearby restaurant for dinner. They were starved. I, on the other hand, lost my appetite after the exchange I had with our waiter. While taking my order, he pointed his finger at me and said with disdain, "You're that guy." I stared back at him and said nothing. I was too paranoid to eat anything off the plate he brought me.

After dinner, we went back to the courtroom, hoping for a decision. The longer it took, the more we worried. It was well after midnight when the jury requested a break for the night.

We convened back in the courtroom the next day. I would learn later that afternoon they could not reach a verdict—the jury was hung. The note they sent back to the judge read, "Hopelessly deadlocked."

My team and I were obviously disappointed and viewed this as a definitive loss. I recall immediately leaving the court room after Judge McKinney announced the verdict. I was taken back to a secluded office within the courthouse. There, I spoke with Danny Overley, a high-ranking department officer who was my trusted mentor. I had finally succumbed to the pressure of the last few months. I broke down. As I sat sobbing, Danny asked, "Would you like for us to look into settlement options so we... so **you** don't have to go through this again?"

"Absolutely not," I replied. I was ready to start over at square one. I wanted to stand firm in my conviction that police officers should be vindicated when justifiable deadly force was used.

I spoke with Danny recently about the trial. He said, "You were just a skeleton back then, just moving around. You just moved from room to room. It was so hard to see it. But you were strong at the same time. You knew you did everything right. But every corner you turned, you had people attacking you."

The rest of the city learned the verdict later that day. *The Star* reported, "A federal judge dismissed a deadlocked jury Saturday after it could not agree whether an Indianapolis police officer violated the rights of robbery suspect Leonard Barnett Jr. during a fatal shooting two years ago. As a result, Officer Scott Haslar faces another trial in federal court."[146] The jury, comprised of five women—one of whom was Black—and one man, could not reach a unanimous decision as needed for a conclusion. The family was seeking over $2.5 million in punitive and compensatory damages.[147]

After the jury deadlocked, Waples and the Barnett family were photographed standing outside on the steps of the federal courthouse, Mary Booker on crutches and a family member holding the photo of Barnett from the trial. "It was not a defeat," Waples said, "and my sense was that it wasn't a single juror holding up a verdict. I think we convinced more than one person that we were right." The court did not disclose how each juror voted.

In response to the verdict, Muhammad Siddeeq was still calling for justice. "We're glad that they just didn't outrightly justify that cold-blooded killing," Siddeeq said. [148]

That entire week turned out to be just a dress rehearsal for the next show. "It's a theatre, Scott," Kautzman said. He went back to the drawing board to discuss a new strategy and decided I needed a new costume. The plan was to soften my look. I was white, blond-haired, blued-eyed—your stereotypical WASP. Dressed in my blue police uniform, I looked too much like a Nazi. (Kautzman compared me to the young boy Rolf from *The Sound of Music* who joins the Third Reich.) They told me to dress in a suit and asked me to grow a beard for the next trial. We also needed to come up with our own board-certified orthopedic surgeon who could testify that Barnett could have walked after the crash.

And there was something else.

We had information about Barnett that we'd been holding back. During preparation discussions for the first trial, we decided it was too delicate of a subject to bring forward. But now that another trial was inevitable, the stakes were higher. We decided to take a risk and introduce a controversial piece of evidence.

Second Trial. The next wave of outrage crested shortly after the first trial. I was promoted to sergeant in January 1993, much to the chagrin of the Concerned Clergy. The front page of the City/State section of *The Star* read, "Pastor blasts promotion of Haslar to sergeant."[149]

I was disheartened.

Promotions of this nature are not subjective. It's simply about passing a test. I studied tirelessly and went through the same objective process as everyone else. My scores landed me third on the overall list of those who passed. But Rev. Harris claimed my new rank was more evidence of the oppression of their community.[150] And this time, he added, "The discrimination also victimizes Blacks within the Indianapolis Police Department." The Concerned Clergy stated, "Several Black policemen were more deserving of promotion than was Patrolman Scott Haslar."[151] The media did not report the fact that the objective, standardized test was created and administered by an independent outside agency.

The day after my promotion was announced, the Concerned Clergy responded with theatrics. *The Star* reported, "Rev. Harris and [Elder Lionel] Rush staged a sketchy reenactment of how they perceived the shooting took place near 10th Street and College Avenue, where Barnett was killed." *The Indianapolis News* ran the following description of the demonstration:

111

Lionel T. Rush pulled out a Black .177-caliber pellet gun and lunged at the Rev. Lucius Newsome. "Bang! Bang! Bang! Bang! Bang!" he shouted. "Call the ambulance to come and get this clown."[152] The Rev. Wayne T. Harris of Mount Olive Missionary Baptist Church pinned two blue paper badges to Rush's chest. One read, "Medal of Valor. Great job, Scott Haslar." The other said, "Sgt."

"Community policing at its best," Rush said sarcastically.[153]

In *The Star*, Chief Toler praised the 26 officers for their scores in the extensive promotional process. But Mayor Goldsmith immediately called for the chief to re-evaluate the process. The article read, "In reference to Toler's decision, Rev. Harris said, 'I love the Black chief. I want him to do good. But… he should have refused to sign his name to an order promoting Scott Haslar.'"[154]

Wayne Voida, the sergeant sent to the scene of my shooting to support me, told me 30 years later, "At that point, I decided I was fed up with the media and protesters giving you shit." On Sunday, February 14, 1993, *The Star* featured a letter to the editor from Voida on the front page of the editorials section. The headline read, "Defending a police officer's promotion."[155]

> The Jan. 30 report, "Pastor blasts promotion of Haslar to sergeant: Decries honor to the officer who shot suspect," is another scathing article directed toward one of my fellow officers, and it fills me with a combination of anger, sadness and dismay.
>
> Rev. Wayne Harris and Elder Lionel Rush, supposedly to illustrate a point, used toy guns and racially sarcastic

comments to conduct a re-enactment of a police action shooting.

First, they demonstrated how totally ignorant they are of the facts of the Leonard Barnett shooting. As has been made well known from all the post-shooting publicity, Officer Haslar is an excellent, dedicated policeman who confronted a dangerous felon in the form of Barnett. Barnett had a number of opportunities to submit to lawful arrest after committing an armed robbery but chose instead to flee officers in a dangerous pursuit and ignore Haslar's command to surrender after wrecking his roommate's Camaro auto and causing near fatal injuries to another of the pursuing officers.

Leonard Barnett was the master of his own destiny, and because of his lawless behavior and unwillingness to comply he is dead.

Second, these "holy men" demonstrate how ignorant they are about the Indianapolis Police Department's promotion process. I am an IPD sergeant. I have participated in this process in order to gain my current rank in the department. I acknowledge that the process is not perfect, but it is fair to all who take part in it. All officers who choose to participate begin with the same study materials, information about the process and opportunity to succeed and obtain a promotion.

Haslar did extremely well in this extensive process, finishing third out of hundreds of candidates who took part in the sergeant promotional examination. His involvement in the Barnett shooting had absolutely nothing to do with his promotion. For Rev. Harris and Elder Rush to indicate otherwise is false and does gross disservice to Haslar, the IPD, the city of Indianapolis and its citizenry.

The shameless publicity-seeking of Harris and Rush serves only to continue racially motivated ill-will generated toward the police department. These ministers take no steps to begin the healing process needed between the Black community and the police department. They make no mention of the fact that Barnett's actions were unlawful, wrong, dangerous and that they ultimately cost him his life.

In fact, by their continuing to eulogize Barnett as a victim, rather than chastise him as a criminal, they can lead impressionable young people to deduce that if they do wrong, these fine ministers will rush to their defense. Apparently Harris and Rush feel that the pigment of one's skin makes one immune from compliance with society's rules. What a foreboding message to send to the young people of our city.

I guess I will just have to sit back with sadness and dismay as these two religious men proclaim good to be evil, and evil to be good.

Jury selection for the second trial began on Monday, February 8. The Barnett family was now seeking $3.5 million in damages instead of the $2.5 million in the first trial.[156] Judge McKinney would once again preside. He encouraged both parties to think about reaching a settlement before going back to trial.[157] The Barnett family was in favor. We were not.

Aside from my team presenting some highly sensitive information about Barnett, our defense strategy hadn't changed much since the first trial. I did, however, make some changes to my appearance. As jury selection began, I sat at the defense table wearing a suit and tie. I agreed to "soften" my look, but I was adamant that I wouldn't grow a beard—that just wasn't me.

There was a vexing addition to this next round. Kautzman informed me that federal courts were looking into a new pilot program—television cameras in the courtroom. I was now on trial and on camera. The media cameramen formed a line with their foreboding lenses. Every move I made was not only being watched by the jury, but by Indianapolis at-home viewers, too.

Prospective jurors were given a hint of our new defense strategy. "You may hear testimony that after Mr. Barnett died, he was given an HIV test," Judge McKinney warned.[158] "The testimony may be that Mr. Barnett tested positive on the HIV test. We will hear testimony on how that may have impacted his life. There will be no testimony on how Mr. Barnett came to test positive on HIV. You are not to speculate on why," he instructed.[159] How he acquired HIV was irrelevant to our defense.

My team didn't want to address the HIV issue in the first trial for two reasons. First, we didn't want it perceived as an attack on the gay community. Second, and more importantly, Kautzman believed we would win based on the merits of my actions alone. But the city was putting pressure on the defense to think about the dollar amount we'd owe in damages if we lost. My team's strategy was to introduce that piece of evidence for one reason: we needed to illustrate that Barnett's life expectancy was shorter than a healthy 25-year-old's would have been, and therefore should be considered in deciding how much money would be awarded.

McKinney also questioned the jurors about their feelings regarding the Rodney King beating in Los Angeles, as well as previous police action shootings by Indianapolis officers. Later that day, after the jury was seated, *The Star* reported, "Retrial opens in civil rights trial against officer: All-white jury selected to hear case."[160] And *The Indianapolis News* jumped in with, "There are no Blacks on the jury and one Black alternate juror."[161]

After a short break, I sat for opening statements in nervous anticipation. This time, however, the extreme anxiety levels seemed familiar—my new normal—despite being on camera. It felt like I was in a bad dream, woke up from it, then fell right back into it.

Waples opened standing next to the large photo of Leonard Barnett. He said, "The critical issue in this trial is whether or not that shooting was legally justified. The evidence you will hear will show that it was not."[162] Waples informed jurors that no gun was ever found, and he argued that Barnett never reached back into the crashed vehicle to look for it. His argument was that I concocted the story about Barnett's actions that night. He said his foot was injured so severely from the crash that he could barely stand, much less run.[163]

In Kautzman's opening statement, he criticized the plaintiff's claim that Barnett could not have walked on his injured leg. He told the jury, "You'll hear evidence later that he could have." He went on to describe Barnett as, "A fleeing suspect with a terminal disease who owed his roommate money."[164] He said I was acting consistently according to policy, the way I was trained. He continued, "Do not allow yourself to get smoke-screened by such things as racial prejudice. It has nothing to do with this case."[165] But race was exactly what the local media landed on. An article in *The Star* the next day read, "Haslar is white; Barnett is Black... A jury of two men and four women, all white, eventually was selected."[166]

We hired our own orthopedic surgeon. Dr. Michael Kaveney testified, "Barnett could have moved around despite a compound fracture to the right ankle which left his shin bone sticking out of the skin. This injury will allow someone to move about. It could even be at a rapid rate."[167]

Herein lies another glaring juxtaposition. Two opposing testimonies offered by similarly trained medical experts. Barnett could not have walked. Barnett could have walked—potentially at a "rapid rate."

Hired guns? It seems that one can find an expert to testify to anything if the price is right. But it could have also been a good-faith disagreement by medical professionals.

But which expert will the jurors listen to, I wondered.

Then the HIV evidence was introduced.

The Indianapolis News reported, "Medical tests showed that slain robbery suspect Leonard Barnett was carrying the virus that causes AIDS, according to a doctor who testified today in the federal lawsuit against the police officer who shot and killed Barnett in 1990." After looking at the results of tests performed on Barnett after his death, Dr. Judith Deutsch testified, "If this were my patient, I would believe he was HIV infected."[168] My defense team knew this tactic was a gamble. How would the jury take this? Would they view it as a homophobic attack? Or, would they see the relevance to Barnett's life expectancy? I remember the collective fear the virus incited within society at that time. Little was known about it, and people largely assumed the diagnosis was a death sentence.

One of the plaintiff's expert witnesses was accountant Michael Skehan. He testified in the first trial as well. *The Indianapolis News* reported, "By one accountant's testimony, holdup suspect Leonard Barnett might have earned nearly $500,000 if he had not been shot to death by Indianapolis Police Officer Scott Haslar on July 9, 1990."[169] A new member of my defense team took that figure to task in her cross examination. "Defense attorney Mary Ann Oldham criticized the figures, saying they were based on the average life-span of Black males, not the shorter life-span Barnett was likely to have because he had contracted HIV. She also objected because Skehan didn't account for the wages Barnett would have lost had he been convicted and sent to prison."[170]

Waples asked Skehan if a positive HIV test would have changed the income estimate. "'No, it wouldn't,' Skehan answered. "When you're dealing with the future, you're dealing with statistics."[171] He testified that a 25-year-old Black man could expect to live another 44 years on average, according to the Indiana Department of Health. That was the number he used to calculate potential earnings. Oldham asked in her cross examination, "If we had a doctor come in to testify that the projected life expectancy of Mr. Barnett was 2 to 20 years, your estimate would be incorrect?"

No, Skehan replied. He said his estimate wouldn't change—even if Barnett had been convicted of robbery and sent to prison.

In closing arguments, Waples again accused me of being deceitful. "He's got to make up a story. Leonard had no motive to go back to the car. None. But Officer Haslar had a motive to lie. You might have sympathy for Officer Haslar. It was a tough position he was put in, no doubt about it. But you are not to be guided by sympathy," he said.[172]

After recapping the week's testimony in his closing statement, Kautzman played a piece of audio for the jury. It was a recording of the police radio traffic from the night of the shooting. He only played a 43-second snippet—when I first got on the radio after the crash until my screeching that I was ok, but "I need a medic for this clown."

I remember wincing at the tone of my voice, sounding so shrill and shaken.

Kautzman asked the jury, "Is that the voice of Clint Eastwood saying, 'Leonard, make my day?' I don't think so," Kautzman said.[173]

The jury received the case around lunchtime.

We walked across the street to eat, wondering if we were in for another excruciating wait. But a few hours later, we got the call—the jury had reached a verdict.

Once again, I was ushered back into the courtroom, a familiar routine by now. After the usual formalities, Judge McKinney asked the foreman if they had reached a unanimous decision. They had. The foreman stood and read the verdict. They had found in favor of the defendant, Sgt. Scott Haslar.

Quiet relief washed over my entire body as Kautzman firmly grabbed my shoulder. As I turned to see the smiles on my team's faces, I caught in my periphery the dropped heads and looks of disgust on the plaintiff's side of the courtroom. I noted another moment of complete juxtaposition in reactions from two opposing sides. We had won; they had lost.

But how very far it was from the truth to think that anyone in this mess had won anything at all.

After the courtroom had mostly cleared, I finally breathed a sigh of relief. I hugged Tammy. I wasn't elated, but I felt some closure. I had hope that I could finally move on.

The Star reported, "The jury of four women and two men deliberated about three hours before finding in favor of IPD Sgt. Scott Haslar, who shot and killed Leonard Barnett Jr. on July 9, 1990." Kautzman's press statement read, "We are absolutely ecstatic. Scott has been living with this stigma over his head for a long time. The community finally vindicated him. He looks forward to a long and happy career as a police officer."[174]

In a follow-up article the next day, Waples said, "It was absolutely the worst time to try this case. That is, (it was) within a week of an [Indiana State] police officer being shot in an unprovoked attack."[175] Waples went on to argue that plaintiffs were at a disadvantage from the start because there were no Black citizens on the jury, despite the alternate who didn't make it to the final deciding panel.

"I guess I would say in the words of my ancestors, it's the same soup warmed over and served on a different day," stated the Rev. Wayne T. Harris. "I would just appeal to the members of the Black community, young and old, to walk diligently," he said. "Stay on the right side of the law, since the life of a Black man in Indianapolis is not worth anything to police. It's been proven over and over again that they will shoot you down if given the chance."[176] The message they're sending our youth, Muhammad Siddeeq concluded, "... is why I believe we are seeing so much lawlessness and anarchy in the streets."[177]

In *The Indianapolis News*, Mmoja Ajabu, organizer of the Indianapolis chapter of the Black Panther Militia, called the verdict a miscarriage of justice. "The verdict tells African Americans that we do not have any rights that the system is bound to respect," he said. Ajabu warned that the decision carried a danger of rioting, much like the Rodney King verdict. The article read, "Ajabu said incidents such as this will cause the Black community to band together and may lead to ethnic violence rivaling that in Bosnia. Instead of dying just because we are Black, we'll be dying for a cause."[178]

After my actions were cleared by a review board, then the coroner, and then later, a grand jury, the family's response was that each of those decisions was just another "rubber stamp" from the system. But I hope at least one thing is evident here. It certainly never felt like I was walking into another automated "rubber stamp" meeting or inquiry, knowing full well I might walk out having been indicted for murder. It also didn't feel that way walking into the federal trials. I knew I could walk out and owe a lifetime of paychecks worth of punitive damages.

To digest and evaluate the actions I took in just 43 seconds of time and space, it took nearly three years of unrelenting media coverage and trial preparations, two separate federal trials spanning two weeks of jury selection and individual testimony, and

18 hours of jury deliberations. But still, it wasn't enough for some segments of the community.

Regardless, it was finally over.

It didn't feel like a vindication. It just felt like a chapter of my life had ended. But as I came to learn, it would never end, not as long as I was still employed by the city of Indianapolis. The future promotions I would receive came with a rekindling of media coverage pointing back to the shooting, which in turn sparked response from the Concerned Clergy. It was a vicious cycle. I wanted to enjoy the success that came with working hard at my job, but I never could. With each new appointment, I braced instead of celebrated.

CHAPTER 7

WHAT IT WAS LIKE

I t's one thing to write about the events of those three years from a strictly informational perspective. "Just the facts, ma'am," as we say in the profession. I can report the details of what happened, quote the headlines, newspaper articles, and evening newscasts. I can reprint the many letters to the editor written about me. I can talk to the people who were there with me and report what they remember. I can tell you what I did and said as best as I can recollect. But none of that illustrates the weight of what I carried and grappled with every day in my own head—that locked-away space to which only I had the key. I would say I gave access to only a few, but even that's an overestimation. Eventually, I learned to self-medicate with alcohol rather than talk to anyone about it.

The problem with this coping mechanism when writing a memoir is that people can help you remember the events, but only you have the answers to what was going on inside of you. And years of active addiction tends to deteriorate the finer details stored in one's brain. Alcohol is a highly effective numbing agent and memory eraser. So, it didn't surprise me when the feedback I received from those who read the first manuscript focused heavily on a lack of adequate personal testimony, i.e., my thoughts and feelings—things that many cops consider a foreign language. My friend Chris said to me, "I'd like to hear more about what it was actually like to be you at that time."

I'll put it concisely. It was fucking hell.

That's easier to say than it is to describe all the situations and circumstances of my everyday life at that time that contributed to and exacerbated my trauma response. And I'm sure that was the case for both parties in this thing—me and the Barnett family. (Lest I give the impression that the misery was one-sided and minimize what they were going through, let me assure you that none of that is lost on me. But I can't tell their story, only mine.)

If I rewind thirty years and try to offer a retrospective based solely on my emotional and psychological experience, it may only amount to bits and pieces of what I remember. Yet it's clear that something is better than nothing in painting the full picture.

The first thing that comes to mind about that time is a piece of this story that, until I began writing, I hadn't talked or thought about since the day it happened. And it's something that I thought was unique to me—an experience I was sure no one else could ever understand, so I pushed it down with the other unprocessed experiences.

I mentioned that at the moment I pulled the trigger, I seemed to briefly come out of body. But what I left out is that all the while, I had some unexplainable knowledge—direct knowledge, if you will—that I would survive. I felt I was watching and controlling my own movements from just above myself. When my consciousness seemed to return to my physical body, I was back to normal.

I had no idea how to talk about this or what it meant, and the mere mention of this notion to my lawyer made him nervous. He wanted to focus on what was legally admissible for my testimony. So, I carried it with me throughout the aftermath of the shooting, sharing it with no one, but always perplexed by it. To experience being the observer and the observed in the same encounter was more than I was able to process on my own. My ideas about my own consciousness up until that point were now turned on their head, but I had a more immediate and real-life situation that needed my attention, so I tucked it away.

In the days following July 9, 1990, as much as I would have loved to crawl into a hole and shut out the things being said about me, it was nearly impossible to live my life in a complete vacuum. I still had to show up and answer to all the boards and inquiries. I was unavoidably privy to the water cooler conversations about me, but I still reported for work every day because I, like everyone else in the country, had bills to pay. Tammy and I were a young couple who started without much, and we were trying to plan for a family. We lived paycheck to paycheck, so taking a leave of absence wasn't an option. I still had to endure the stares and condemning looks from those who recognized me in public.

My alcoholism surfaced slowly and insidiously. It didn't come on all at once. As soon as I was reassigned to the shooting range, I developed my first addictive coping mechanism: exercise. And the way I exercised was not normal or healthy. I started working out at least two times a day. I'd get an intense workout in when I got to the range. When I got home, I'd go for a run. Sometimes, I'd even go back out for another run. It was all I could do to help channel the anxiety and paranoia that was descending on my psyche. Tammy remembers that while I had started drinking more, at that point, it was still in check. The constant exercise was what I used to quell the inner turmoil. I dropped nearly 25 pounds in the next few months.

I should have taken that veteran officer's advice and stopped paying attention to the news. But in the first few days after the event, I would hunker down with Tammy after work, watch the news, and talk through what was happening. Once the reports, as Tammy put it, "stopped being factual," we turned it off. She said I would become so upset that neither of us could tolerate it. Still, it was hard not to at least take a peek when my own personal public train wreck was the local top story. At times, I couldn't resist the urge. But the advice I received not to bother always turned out to be sound.

Though I was functioning in the first weeks after the shooting, inside I did not feel functional. I felt as if the world was against me, like I was alone on an island, attacks coming from all sides. The news reports continued spiraling, and I realized I had absolutely no control over what was being said. I had no way of getting my side of the story out there.

We tried to keep moving and living our lives as best we could with the near-constant media coverage and trial preparations. When Tammy got pregnant, I started to worry about money, so I took on part-time work. I wanted to make up for lost income associated with my assignment to day shift, which meant a lower rate of pay. Occasionally, I worked off-duty security, sometimes at the Indy 1500 Gun & Blade Show.

As a Second Amendment advocate, I'm fully aware that events like this are potential petri dishes for the cultivation of anti-gun philosophy. Maybe it's changed since then, but I witnessed gun owners who claimed to be responsible and educated ejecting live ammunition from guns that were required to be unloaded before entrance in front of me at the security safety table.

One weekend as I walked the gun show floor, I was approached by a middle-aged white male in a sea of many. He said, "Officer Haslar, I know who you are and I know what you stand for." He handed me a pamphlet and said, "Take a look at it and join us," before disappearing into the crowd. The literature was about a New World Order conspiracy theory and Zionist Occupation Government. I didn't even know what that was back then. After recently doing some research, I learned the common theme of New World Order theories is the belief that a clandestine power elite, or cabal, is attempting to rule the world through an authoritative government. Around the time of my shooting, this far-right thought was advocated by two distinct groups—militant anti-government and fundamentalist Christians fearing the ultimate end and return of the Antichrist. The literature had an air of hatred and suggested violence toward specific races and religions.

As I thought about the encounter with that man, I realized the way I was portrayed in the media led some of these groups to conclude I was "one of them."

This was a very unsettling thought. The man who handed me that pamphlet, so sure he knew my mind and heart, couldn't have been further from the truth. Can you imagine me as that rookie officer first starting my career—the guy who wanted to save the victims of his community—now being perceived as one of these hate-mongers? I was devastated by how misunderstood I felt. Helpless and hopeless are two words that come to mind.

This was when extreme paranoia set in.

For the most part, I exclusively left my house to go to work. I returned home as soon as the day was over—the only place I felt any semblance of safety. I changed my route home almost every night, taking different roads and unnecessary turns, many times going completely out of my way.

I went to great lengths to conceal our identity. I made sure we were no longer listed in the phone book. This was before the internet. Back then, if a person took the right steps, he could still control how much public information was available about him. I wouldn't throw a single piece of our mail away. I destroyed it. I didn't want anyone to know where we lived.

I wouldn't mow the yard without disguising myself in a hat and sunglasses, and I'd turn my head every time a car or pedestrian passed. I stopped shopping at my normal grocery store, and I hid every distinguishable feature I could while out in public. I was constantly worried that someone would identify me. My wife and I avoided going out to dinner or public outings, and when we did, we left as soon as someone recognized me.

Sitting through the trials and listening to Waples' descriptions, or assumptions, of how the shooting happened, not to mention how he portrayed my character, was its own sort of hell. It's hard to hear yourself characterized as a villain when what you'd been aiming for was a hero. It made me sad. But moreover, it made me angry. I had no way of defending myself or correcting the lies and inaccuracies as I sat at the defense table. I couldn't make statements to the media, nor were they asking for them.

I was called a liar over and over again when I knew in my bones I had been forthright. It began to warp my opinion of myself and eat away at my self-esteem little by little. At some point, maybe after the trials, I started to believe I was that person they said I was for those three years—a shadow that I used the bottle to avoid confronting.

The day before closing arguments of the first trial, Tammy's stepfather, who was in the courtroom every day with the rest of my family, suffered a heart attack. As we braced ourselves for the jury to begin deliberations the next day, he was undergoing quadruple bypass surgery. *And in two days, we might be losing our house and filing for bankruptcy,* I was thinking. We were under enormous stress as we worried about her parents, as well as the end of the proceedings and what it might bring for us.

I went into the second trial thinking I was used to the whole media circus, but the cameras in the courtroom opened up a whole new portal of angst. *Because I'm just not getting enough quality time in the media,* I thought sardonically.

The genesis of "The Look," as I refer to it now, was in that courtroom. It describes the familiar sting of the visceral reactions I invoked in others. When Waples said something negative about me, the jury would, in unison, shift their inquisitive gaze from him to me, piercing me with a look of apparent collective disdain.

Eventually I grew accustomed to, but not fond of, The Look. If I had to describe it, I'd say it's an expression that progresses from shock, to fear, and often times, to contempt. It's usually followed with judgement absent the facts. Most often, it surfaces during conversations about my policing career when I'm directly questioned and admit that I killed someone in the line of duty. I always tried to avoid the topic because of it.

I taught Social Problems and Community Policing at the University of Indianapolis for several years. Sometimes I would see The Look on a student's face, prompting me to ask, "Did you Google me?"

Sometimes, one's morbid curiosity would get the best of them, inspiring the dreaded question, "What does it feel like to kill someone?"

Most people would naturally assume that one feels guilt and shame. But how would any of them ever really know what it would or should feel like? Most of them have never been in that situation, but in their ignorance of the experience, they judge those who have because of what they've been taught or conditioned to believe. Even the vast majority of police officers don't know what it's like to kill someone—it's not as common as the media and entertainment industry lead you to believe.

The truth that's hard to hear is that when your lethal actions are in response to a perceived and/or immediate threat to your life, guilt does not necessarily follow. You might feel bad about it overall. You might wish the other person hadn't lost their life. But you may not feel guilty. For those who were raised under the strict doctrine, "Thou shalt not kill," it may come immediately (like a friend of mine you'll read about later). How one feels about taking another's life is subjective and personal—there's no right way to respond. But I've been told for the last three decades that the way I responded was wrong.

After the tumultuous media onslaught, I started feeling guilty for not feeling guilty. This leads to shame, a completely useless emotion. Guilt suggests I did something wrong, whereas shame suggests that I AM something wrong. Shame leads to deleterious coping strategies, including isolation and self-medication.

For years after the trial ended, my name would find its way back into print news every now and then, which reignited the memories and anxiety, likely contributing to chronic stress.

I was mentioned in an article five years after the shooting. My name was used to prove the point that the recent death of a white person at the hands of police didn't receive the same amount of attention as the Barnett shooting.

In 1998, *The Star* ran a featured letter to the editor about suspects killed by police in the line of duty. After a brief recap of my shooting, the author wrote, "Several months later, Haslar received an award for bravery in shooting an unarmed, broken-legged Black man."[179] Eight years had passed, and still those descriptions surfaced and sucker punched me. I got used to my co-workers saying, "Hey, saw your name again in the paper." Drinking was the only refuge I had on those days.

Here I am all these years later, and the memories, PTSD, and worst of all, The Look, still haunt me. Though I'm consistently reticent in discussing that part of my life with anyone, I have allowed myself to get close to one or two new friends. One of them, Robert, I met in a meditation class I attended regularly. We found we had several outside interests in common, including biking.

One day after a ride, we sat talking at a coffee shop. The conversation turned to the current police/community conflict, and despite that inner vise-grip that usually stops me from opening up to someone, I told him about the shooting. And there it was on his face, like an old nemesis returned from a long hiatus. I was sure that was the last I'd hear from him.

I'm happy to report that Robert and I are still friends. He later admitted that he was in shock that day at the coffee shop. He said he mulled it over and processed our conversation for days. And inevitably, he Googled me. But, he said, after sifting through all the information out there, taking in the negative things written about me and my character, he finally said to himself, "That's not the guy I met." Unfortunately, not everyone has that reaction.

All of this to say that my experiences then are not all that different than today. I continue to mostly keep to myself. That 43 seconds in the summer of 1990 that ended a life will forever color the rest of my life.

CHAPTER 8

CONTROVERSIAL CAREER

AFTER THE SHOOTING

I can't recall exactly when my dance with suicidal ideation began. It was sometime after I was exonerated following my second federal trial, not before. Prior to the verdict, I had focused all my psychic energy on clearing my name. The feeling of transitory elation after hearing the verdict was short-lived. "Keep your eye on the prize," was the mindset I used to propel myself through those difficult years. I was just trying to focus on clearing my name. After it was all over, I realized my hard-won exoneration was no prize at all. I slowly began to meltdown. Tammy said she witnessed me change into a very different man. She said, "I think back to when we first got married and you got your job. I remember how happy you were to go to work. I've never seen anyone so happy to go to a job in my life. That joy you got from your career went away, and I never saw that come back."

My drinking increased as I navigated the second half of my life—after the shooting. What followed were a series of career moves that set me on a path of promotions, all against the backdrop of my internal struggles with ending my life and drinking. Some of the jobs weren't quite the right fit, but when I moved on to one that was, I was able to immerse myself in work during the day while trying to manage my inner demons at night. In a job with many inherent stresses, I often found myself jumping into the fire and helping manage other people's well-being while mine was not in great shape.

As a newly promoted sergeant, I no longer had the privilege of the FOP-negotiated contractual rights the street officer enjoyed, like the ability to bid for shift or assignment preference. I was now considered part of management. That meant I could be assigned anywhere in the department at the chief's discretion.

One of my first assignments was Case Management—a unit that no longer exists. Its function was to centralize and track all of the detectives' assignments in a computerized system. I knew little if anything about being a detective at the time, and even less about computers. I couldn't even type. But they didn't want me on the street, so they had to put me somewhere.

I would go weekly to the Deputy Chief of the Investigations Division and ask for a new assignment.

One day, he called me into his office. He said, "I know it's not a street assignment, but would you be interested in heading up a squad over at the Metropolitan Drug Task Force?" This was an independent joint task force of officers from IPD, as well as officers from outlying cities and counties, assigned to conduct drug operations. Investigators worked closely with the DEA and other federal agencies in pursuit of major targets.

I was ecstatic. I was out of Case Management. I would get to be the police again.

Some in the unit were offended that I was given that assignment with no experience in narcotics investigations. Looking back, they should have been. The others had paid their dues in street-level narcotics units before being assigned to a coveted spot in Metro Drug. Some thought I didn't earn the assignment. I was just being appeased. I tried hard to fit in and learn the job. Unfortunately, I wasn't very good at it. Undercover work takes a different breed. You have to be able to play a character very different than the person you are—something I was never able to master.

In the fall of 1995, Chief Toler stepped down. Assistant Chief of Police Donald Christ moved into the top spot. With a new guy in power, I requested yet again to move back to the street in uniform. Finally, Chief Christ assigned me to South District Late Tactical Shift from 7 p.m. to 3 a.m. I was back to working at night, where I felt more comfortable.

It was around this time my drinking started ramping up. I was glad I was back on the street, but it also began taking its toll. Every co-worker, every corner, every radio run seemed to remind me of those painful years between 1990 and 1993. Tammy was on day shift, working as the director of nursing at a medical facility. I'd get home while she and Madi were asleep. I would drink hard for an hour or two and then sleep until noon. I was able to hide it for the most part, even as it accelerated.

A year after I was back on the street, I was transferred to the full-time SWAT Commander position. In that capacity, I oversaw operations of SWAT personnel, training, and logistics. It was an administrative position.

The last thing I wanted to do was leave the street after waiting so long to get back there.

"Why me," I asked my teammates in a meeting.

"Because no one else wants to do it," was the reply. Some endorsement.

Kicking and screaming, I took the job.

I've been involved in serving well over a hundred felony warrants and call-ups during my career, many long since forgotten. During my short time as the SWAT commander, however, there was one call-up I've never forgotten, and never will. The experience found a place in my psyche alongside killing Leonard Barnett. Another indelible mark on my soul.

On March 11, 1999, SWAT was requested to assist with a hostage situation at 4020 North Cornelius Ave. It was brutally cold outside. The snow was layered nearly a foot deep from a recent front that had just blasted the city. North District officers received a radio run—a possible criminal abduction. The victim, whose name was Gina, was walking with a friend when they were approached by the suspect. An argument ensued and the suspect grabbed Gina by the arm and pulled her off into an alley. The police were called.

Since we didn't know Gina's location, responding officers requested a K9 unit to assist. They started from the point of the abduction and tracked through the deep snow, the K9 quickly picking up Gina's unique fear scent. The dog led the team to the rear of a vacant duplex. The door was slightly ajar. The officers entered the house yelling, "Police and dog!" They heard a woman cry out,

"Don't come any closer! He's got a gun! He'll kill me!" They backed out of the house, set up perimeters, and called for a street supervisor, who requested SWAT.

A true hostage situation—not a common event—and I was the SWAT Commander.

Responding SWAT officers did their thing. Snipers were deployed to their snowy hides. The entry team leader took control; an emergency entry team formed while a detailed plan was put together to save the hostage (known as a deliberate hostage rescue). Command level personnel arrived at the scene as well as hostage negotiators. For those not familiar with SWAT operations, a call-up is a balancing act between this trifecta—command level personnel who decide if and when to go, negotiators doing their best to talk the suspect out peacefully, and SWAT warriors ready to liberate the hostage.

During the initial stages of any call-up, we gather as much intelligence as possible to gain insight into the dynamics of the situation we're trying to resolve. As I recall now, we weren't sure of the suspect's identity initially. We understood that he was possibly homeless and had been seen in the area stalking the victim, who had a minor criminal history, including a prostitution offense. To my disappointment, this became a topic of debate among the negotiators. They threw out theories like, "Could this just be a John who's angry over a previous business transaction?"

My contention was—who gives a shit what her criminal history looks like? Right now, she's one thing and one thing only—a hostage. James Gray, an old SWAT buddy of mine, was second in line on that particular entry team—the team leader's wing man. He and I talked about this call-up recently. He remembers the conversation about the victim's profession. "I don't condone what they said. They don't get to see what humans are capable of on a regular basis. These people get disconnected from the reality of evil. If it was your daughter in there, you'd risk it. I guarantee that," he said, agreeing with my position.

We intuitively knew this was not going to end well if we didn't do something fast. Despite our best efforts, we failed to make verbal contact with the suspect. He never said a word to us, so we couldn't negotiate a surrender. SWAT personnel in the profession today would recognize this as a crisis situation, not a hostage situation. We heard the victim screaming for help. Snipers on the perimeter could hear her pleas. The gravity of the situation intensified rapidly. I heard from several seasoned SWAT veterans on the team, "This one's bad, boss! We need to do something." In my ten years on the team, I couldn't recall a single instance where the subject wouldn't communicate with us at all.

"I know," I told the team. "I'm doing my best. Just make sure the boys are ready for an entry and fast." During that era, the SWAT commander didn't make the call to go. The deputy chief made the call. He wasn't ready to send us in, so all we could do was wait and prepare for a rescue.

Fitz (the officer who started the standing ovation when I received the medal of valor) remembers this call-up all too well. He was now on SWAT and was still an FNG, or "fucking new guy." He reluctantly took the assignment I gave him of gathering information on call-ups.

We were experimenting with new audio technology. Fitz crawled up close enough to the house to place a microphone just inside the door. He said, "You could hear her for hours. She was crying and begging for us to come in there and help her. You could hear her whimpering. You never heard a peep from him. That was the eerie thing."

Once Fitz put the listening devices in place and wired audio back to the van, command personnel actually heard the victim's voice. They understood the gravity of our concern then, and we were cleared for a tactical rescue.

But it was too late. Just as we were given the OK to proceed, we heard a gunshot. Fitz remembers hearing the victim say, "You shot me!" Then another shot.

That's when my guys went in. Gray still remembers this moment. "First shot, boom, we're moving. On the way up, I hear a second shot. So my instant thought was—body recovery. Murder suicide. It's all over. I was still in business (mode), but I thought it was over," he said. But the suspect was still very much alive and armed with a two-shot Deringer. Gray remembers the next few minutes all too well.

After breaching the door, the team moved from the front to the rear, where the kitchen was located. Just before entering the kitchen, Gray noticed the basement door. He recalled:

What I first saw was her lying halfway down the stairs. Face up. Her head was in a crawl space. I knew she was dead. I see the dude at the bottom of the stairs. First I heard him speak all night, and it was exactly the cliché, 'Fuck you, coppers!' Saw the gun and thought, is that a gun? Is he pointing a gun at me?" That's when the suspect fired a round, which hit the step just below Gray. He said, "Safety off, I'm starting to shoot." When you're scared, you can crank rounds really fast. So I start shooting... 1-2-3-4, about 5 rounds into it. He just stood there. I thought, *oh my god, I'm missing. I'm missing. Nothing's happening. He's not falling down like he's supposed to.* I got worried I was missing

This reminded me of Barnett—I just didn't think I'd hit him. People make assumptions of what a body's reaction looks like when directly hit by gunfire based on TV and movies. The reality is, that just isn't accurate.

Gray's wing man was on the other side of the basement door returning fire as well. "I roll back in. Dude had his foot on one step like he's walking up at me. And he's taken multiple rounds. Now he starts to crumple. The systems just begin to collapse, and the person sort of corkscrews into the ground. They just fall down slowly. Game over. We're finished."

All these years later, Gray offered me an interesting perspective—a completely opposite assessment than mine. He said, "A portion of the operation was a failure in that she died. But it was not for a lack of the team or SWAT command, as we were prepared. And you were advocating for a rescue. The entry and the fight were a success in that we accomplished the mission once they allowed you to let us go." Gray was able to separate Gina from the event for psychological reasons. His role started after her life had ended. My role, on the other hand, started while she was still alive.

For the last 22 years, I've seen it as a complete failure.

Two opposing views of the same operation show the subjectivity of an individual's trauma response.

To this day, I wonder if I had done enough to convince command personnel of the gravity of that situation. What if we got in before she'd been shot? Would she still be alive today? If she had to die then and there, I wish she could have heard the doors blow off the hinges and the team scream, "Police!" At least then, she would have died knowing she was worthy of being rescued.

She was the only hostage the team had ever lost, and all these years later, I still hold myself accountable. I have often wondered, if this had happened in a white, affluent neighborhood, would it have ended differently?

I left the full-time SWAT commander position to go back to South District but stayed on the team. Mainly I just wanted to be back on the street again, taking radio runs with the troops. But eventually the guilt and shame—deserved or not—consumed me. My drinking continued to get worse, although I was the consummate professional at keeping it in the closet.

I continued my battle with suicidal ideation. Tammy and I were on opposite shifts again. I would get home after a night on the streets around 3:30 a.m. and start drinking while she was still in bed. Before I was up the next day, she had already gotten Madi to the babysitter and was off to work. I would pick Madi up later in the afternoon and spend time with her. Often, Tammy and I would meet in a parking lot on my way back to work at night to trade Madi.

I started conducting traffic stops alone, even when I was picking up on danger cues. At times, I found myself wishing I would be killed in the line of duty. I was making stops in the hood. I wouldn't notify control or ask for backup. I would wonder, will this be the night? If I were killed, I thought, at least Tammy and Madi would be taken care of financially. Funds are set up for the families of officers who die in the line-of-duty. I remember that dark place I lived in far too well.

Many officers have photos of loved ones—spouses, partners, kids—on the dashboard of their patrol cars. (It's our office.) For several years, I had a photo of Madi on my dash. It was my favorite silhouette shot of her from her shoulders up, beautiful eyes and big bright smile. Those were the "eyes of chance" I referenced in Solitude's Last Dance, a poem I'd written about my ongoing waltz with suicidal ideation. (see Appendix I). I was trying to anchor myself to life and the things that mattered most. After each run, I would get back into my car and ground myself by looking at her photo.

Not today. That was the mantra that ran through my head as I stared into her eyes and willed myself to stay in this life. *Not today*.

I bought a new bicycle to take my mind off things. I loved to ride. Getting lost on the road had a sort of spiritual component for me. I started training for a century, or a 100-mile ride. This gave me a distant goal to focus on.

I remember a particularly dark day soon after my purchase. Tammy was out of town on business, and I had taken Madi to the babysitter, where I knew she was safe. Back at home, I sat on my couch in the living room with my pistol in front of me on the ottoman. I was contemplating blowing my brains out.

My bike or my gun?

Once again, I convinced myself to live. I decided to go for a ride. I spent two hours pedaling to clear my head.

Not long after Tammy got home from her business trip, I was back in the same dark place. One day while she was at work, I called her in tears and said we needed to talk. We met in a Walmart parking lot. She recalls I was in rough shape. I told her I was thinking about killing myself. She made an appointment for me to see a psychiatrist right away. She also asked me to make a safety contract with her right then and there in the parking lot. I promised I wouldn't do anything before I'd had a chance to get some help.

The psychiatrist put me on medication. She also suggested I begin therapy, but I had no desire to talk to anyone. I was embarrassed by my suicidality. I also started seeing a holistic nurse practitioner who was trying to help me make lifestyle changes with diet and exercise. But I was continuing to drink heavily, so none of these interventions had a chance to prove helpful. I continued in and out of dark moods and even darker thoughts. I envisioned how I would kill myself over and over again. I ruminated on my plan, and the idea that everyone in my life would be better off without me.

Then came the year 2000. I remember New Year's Eve 1999 very well. It fell on a day that should have been one of my days off, but SWAT personnel were all ordered to work. The administration wanted the team staged at the downtown heliport in case all hell broke loose at the stroke of midnight of the year 2000. The collective national fear that echoed in the news those days sounded like Armageddon—the end of humanity as we knew it.

The ball dropped and nothing happened. I sat there at midnight and watched several transformers explode in an eerie glow in the sky—taken out by people celebrating the New Year with high-powered rifles. The computer systems turned out to be smarter than the humans. They continued to do the right thing.

In the early part of the decade, I studied and tested for the lieutenant's test. I did well in the process, got promoted, and was assigned to South District Late Shift. Fitz was one of my shift sergeants.

The suicidal ideation storms came in waves—both crests and troughs. But never did the gravity of suicide hit home quite as hard as it did in July of 2001. In my career, I had been at the scene of many tragic suicides and felt the pain of their loved ones, but never had I been named in anyone's suicide note.

One of my late-shift officers was getting himself into some trouble while in uniform. I knew he was also having problems at home. I needed to have a talk with Jerry. I pulled him from his regular duties one night to keep him out of trouble. This was just the beginning of a disciplinary process for him. Fitz contacted me that same night and said Jerry was ready to talk to me about his issues, but I was already home at that point. The shift was busy, and there just wasn't time earlier in the night. "Tell him I'll meet with him tomorrow," I said.

The next night, Jerry wasn't at roll call. Fitz remembers another one of our guys running in from the back, yelling at us to get outside.

Jerry drove to work in his police car, dressed in uniform. He parked in the back lot, typed out a suicide note on his laptop, then put his gun to his head and pulled the trigger. He was removed from his car by responding medics. I remember seeing him lying on the ground. It was obvious it was too late for CPR. He was clearly gone. As I looked at his lifeless, mangled body, I felt a pang of guilt. I should have talked to him. It also occurred to me for a brief moment—*this is what I'd look like if I chose to do this.*

Not today, I thought. *Not today.*

We stood over his dead body there on the concrete. That's when Fitz looked at me and said, "You think you were a little too hard on him?" Cop humor—one of the many dysfunctional coping mechanisms we develop.

After investigators completed, I told Fitz to take his stuff out of the car. Fitz recalls opening the laptop and finding his suicide note. One of the first lines read, "Lt. Haslar, I wish we could have met sooner, because I was much stronger then." He was ready to talk the night before, but the shift was just too busy. By the next night, his mental health had deteriorated to the point of committing suicide. What if I had driven back to work that night and met with him? Would he still be alive today?

I was completely lost at this point in life. Professionally, my career was still on the rise. Personally, I was headed into the gutter. My marriage to Tammy was slowly deteriorating. I began detaching from Tammy after the shooting drama ended, and we never found our way back to each other. Our relationship devolved from partners into something more akin to roommates. My job no longer made me happy. Home didn't make me happy. The only thing I looked forward to was drinking after work so I could erase the internal madness and pain I was feeling. In desperation, I started looking outside of myself and my family to find relief. Alcohol worked, but I was lonely. I found myself seeking female attention outside of my marriage.

I started seeing Julie, a fellow officer, after work hours behind Tammy's back. Initially, it was for a drink here and there. Eventually, we started sleeping together. In 2004, I found out she was pregnant. The pressure of this news was too much for my marriage to withstand. My son Matthew was born in November of 2004. A short time later, Tammy and I divorced. The next few years involved a series of tumultuous legal battles with Julie that I endured so I could be in my son's life. I had little to show for myself financially after all was said and done. I was incredibly depressed and lost, but I continued showing up for work. I was navigating a contentious co-parenting situation with a new son while trying to maintain a good relationship with my daughter, who was in her early teens. I felt like I was failing miserably. The drinking, my only crutch, continued.

On May 19, 2007, my parents' neighbor called me to tell me my dad had taken a fall and was unconscious. My intuition told me Dad was gone. When I got to the house, I found him lifeless at the top of the stairs. The next three days, I was slam drunk.

I remember attending a funeral once with dad when I was in high school. As we were viewing his friend's body, someone came up to Dad and said, "Doesn't he look good?" As we were leaving, he turned to me and said, "Do me a favor, son. When that's me someday lying there in the casket, don't tell anyone I look good. You don't look good. You're dead." Well, Dad, I'm here to tell you—you looked terrible at the top of the stairs that day.

I know now I didn't take enough time to grieve my dad. We buried him, and life just went on. But something that has stayed with me all these years is the fact that I hadn't talked to my dad in more than a week before he died. Our normal day to catch up on the phone was Sunday. But the week prior to his death, I was so busy with work that I neglected to make that Sunday afternoon phone call. I'll live with that regret forever.

Not long after, I was asked to take over the Street Level Enforcement Detail (SLED) team. This was a unit comprised of the most proactive and productive police officers with which I've ever had the privilege of working. SLED was tasked with patrolling the most crime-ridden areas of the city. Arrests and gun seizures were the measure of success. It was the only group of individuals I ever supervised where at the end of the shift, you had to tell them, "Stop working and go home. Please."

David Moore was a SLED team member. He was like the little brother I never had. Both of his parents, Jo and Spencer, were career police officers with the city. David was still in high school when I met them. He was interested in following in their footsteps. Jo asked me if I would take him on a ride-along, which I was happy to do. We hit it off immediately, and he rode with me several more times. I trained David in the martial arts before he was hired by the police department, not knowing one day he would work directly under me.

I was the first responding SLED supervisor to the scene the night David shot and killed an alleged gang member in November of 2008. He heard shots fired and got out of his car to investigate. At a backyard party, two individuals were in a fight over a gun.

147

David ordered them to drop the weapon. One of them let go. The one now in control of it turned and pointed it directly at David, who fired in self-defense.

I arrived shortly after, the smell of burnt gun powder still lingering, and immediately took control of the scene. I knew all too well what to do. I walked David to my car, helped to calm him down, and instructed him not to say anything to anyone until John Kautzman arrived. He had the same look on his face I probably did on that early July morning in 1990: What the fuck just happened? As his immediate supervisor and friend, I checked in on him throughout the aftermath. He was doing as well as anyone could be after taking a life. But like me, David was a very private person. He kept his cards close to his chest. If he struggled, he never shared it with me.

In 2009, I left SLED to become the East District crime strategist at the request of the new East District Commander. The Eastside notoriously had some of the most violent areas in the city. In that position, I was responsible for the development and supervision of crime reduction efforts. The commander and I were somewhat progressive by industry standards and were willing to try anything if it made the Eastside safer.

I read and researched a great deal. I was introduced to some new crime reduction efforts that showed great promise in other areas of the country, one of which was the High Point Drug Market Intervention (DMI) in North Carolina. The other was the Baker One Domestic Violence Intervention Project developed in Charlotte-Mecklenburg, NC.

The DMI targets open-air drug markets and the violence associated with those areas. Our first target was located near 38th and Post Road in several apartment complexes.

The protocol is to send in undercover officers over a period of time to make controlled buys off as many targets as possible. During this process, each suspect is classified as being on an A or B list, based on their prior criminal history. Those with violent criminal histories were placed on the A list, or those we would attempt to prosecute to the fullest extent of the law. They often went on to serve lengthy sentences in prison. Those who had minor criminal histories with no violent or prior gun charges were placed on the B list and were given a second chance. All those on the B list were instructed to come into East District roll call to see the evidence we had regarding their narcotics trafficking. Often, the evidence was overwhelming, including video and audio of each of the buys we made from them.

At the end, we agreed to not follow through with prosecution if they signed a contract stating that they would not sell dope or engage in any serious criminal activity, including possession of firearms, in the future. We held the evidence for the length of the statute of limitations for the offense they committed. If they stayed on course, no charges would ever be filed. If they violated the contract, we filed the charges and they would be looking at prison time if convicted. In the first DMI, we had around 30 targets, only four of which were offered the deal. They all took it.

One day, I got a call from Fitz, who was now assigned to the Great Lakes Regional Task Force with the U.S. Marshalls. He wanted to interview targets on the A list to see if he could obtain information on other criminal activity. His unit was trying to turn them into state's informants to go after bigger targets. Fitz, who was always slightly skeptical of my progressive crime-reduction ideas, called me after interviewing one of the A-listers and said, "This is a great concept, boss, but I just talked to a guy sitting in jail who should have fallen onto the B list. He has no priors. And he's kind of a nice guy. Doesn't seem your system worked out too well for him."

That can't be, I thought. I checked those criminal histories extensively. *Oh shit. Did we arrest the wrong dude?*

In a panic, I immediately went to my narcotics guys and confirmed. We arrested the right target, but I pulled the wrong criminal history. Both were young Black males that had addresses in the focused area. They had common first and last names but different middle initials and birth dates. I screwed up. This guy had a very minor criminal history—the other guy's was extensive and violent.

After one deep breath, I knew what I had to do.

I showed up at his next pretrial hearing to talk with his defense attorney and the deputy prosecutor. This guy had been sitting in jail since his arrest. If convicted, he was looking at possibly the next 20 years in prison. He was young and had children at home he was trying to support. I explained everything to the defense attorney. He looked at me stunned.

"So, what you're saying is that you want to drop all the charges on my client right here and now if he agrees to not engage in future serious criminal behavior or carry guns?"

"Yeah," I replied.

"I've been doing defense work for over twenty years, and I've never heard anything like this before in a pretrial," he said.

He talked to his client. The young man was processed and released later that day. In the next DMI we conducted, I asked this young man to talk to those on the B list and tell his story, which he was more than happy to do. He did such a great job in those conversations. I'm sure he changed some lives. I often wonder how he's doing today. Had he been convicted, he might still be in prison. I think today's system would benefit from having more incentive programs like this available.

In August 2010, my boss was promoted to deputy chief of Operations. I was appointed East District commander by my former academy classmate, now chief of police, Paul Ciesielski, to continue our progressive initiatives. While I was thrilled about the promotion, I knew it meant more media attention and digging up the past. I sat down with the chief and the director of Public Safety to prepare for the press conference that was scheduled to announce the promotion.

The Star's article the next day read, "New leader named for East District." Reporter Jon Murray wrote, "After the 1990 shooting, Black ministers and others protested for several weeks, with some activists suggesting Barnett's race—he was Black—played a role in the shooting... He weathered community leaders' accusations of brutality and racism, and he won a jury verdict in a civil rights suit filed by the victim's family. He emerged with career intact, and he has quietly risen through the police ranks since."[180]

Richard Waples, the Barnett family's attorney in the federal trials, was asked for a comment. He said my promotion gave him pause, but, he said, "People learn and grow too. I don't know Haslar today... We had our day in court, and we didn't prevail, and he did. I think the department can take that result and move forward."[181]

Now that it was 2010, the information regarding the Barnett shooting was no longer contained just in print media. The internet was a thing now, and this promotion was the news vehicle that officially put the story on the World Wide Web. *WTHR* ran an online story titled, "New East District Commander Addresses 1990 Shooting."[182] In it, Chief Ciesielski said I was promoted in part because of a 30% decrease in violent crime in the East District since that January.

When asked about the shooting, I was quoted as saying, "It is something that will always be in the back of my mind. I moved on. I was exonerated by several courts back then, civil trials, an FBI investigation and I have gone on to a fairly successful career and that is what I am focusing on now. Where I'm going in the future, not the past."[183]

I wrote bullet points to address questions about the shooting, but I didn't have a rehearsed response. Looking back today, I feel pretty good about that response, but it occurs to me how much emotion I was repressing so I could make statements like that. A part of me was still focused on the past, regardless of the sound bite I had to give them.

The Rev. James Jackson, pastor of Fervent Prayer Church and head of the Far Eastside Action Coalition (F.E.A.C.), attended my promotion ceremony. He complimented our progressive crime-prevention projects and our partnership with the community. I was very fond of Rev. Jackson. We worked closely together in that community. He said to the media, "It is one thing to question one's integrity, but then you have to go forward and prove he had no integrity. Apparently, it was proven Commander Haslar does have integrity."[184]

Mmoja Ajabu, an Indianapolis minister and the former commander in chief of the Black Panther Militia, hosts an "International Action Against Police Brutality"[185] website, *Ajabu Speaks*. While the site's description reads, "A voice of truth to increase the love and decrease the hate,"[186] Ajabu's postings, in my opinion, tend to encourage violence against police and other positions of authority within the government as a response to what he and his community perceive as injustices against Black people.

In an Indianapolis Monthly article, Ajabu served notice to governmental officials that if conditions for Blacks didn't improve by the end of the year, the militia would go on the offensive and bloodshed would ensue. He said, "We believe that revolution is the solution."[187] He posted a department photo of me in uniform on his site along with the following summary of my promotion: "The above officer, Scott Haslar, shot and killed Leonard Barnett. Leonard was unarmed, had been in a car accident which broke his leg into two pieces, and as he was getting out of the wreck was shot to death by Scott Haslar. Because Haslar killed Leonard he was given a medal and promoted to be the East Commander of the Indianapolis Police Department."[188] I couldn't help but wonder if Ajabu's call to arms would bring violence in my direction.

On Sunday, January 23, 2011, I received a staff page that an officer had been shot during a traffic stop near 34th and Temple Ave. It was David Moore, my adopted little brother. During the stop, the suspect jumped from his vehicle and ambushed David. *The Star* reported, "As one of their own fought for his life Sunday, Indianapolis investigators searched for clues as to why officer David Moore was shot—four times, twice in the head—during a morning traffic stop."[189]

I found myself once again frustrated with the media. I couldn't imagine what clues our investigators could possibly come up with that would somehow explain "why" this ambush occurred. David would have given the very shirt off his back if he thought it would help someone on the street in need.

The Star spoke with Indianapolis pastor Rev. Harry Spigner. He heard the shots fired as he was sitting in his office preparing for his morning sermon at a nearby church. Later, he walked to the scene to comfort and pray alongside responding officers who came to him when they saw his clerical collar.[190]

Making sense of such a cold-blooded act is impossible and maddening.

Rev. Spigner offered his solace. "The first message is prayer for the individual. We really lifted up the other officers, and the perpetrator too… Because it's really about community, and so we pray for peace. We know that he stood between us and the bad guy, and our hearts are full for him and his family."[191]

Upon hearing the news, I immediately put my uniform on and started driving around the Eastside, looking for the suspect's vehicle. After no luck, I drove directly to the hospital. There, I saw David lying in an ICU bed, fighting for his life. He was hooked up to a plethora of machines with tubes coming out of his body. I stood there as his sister arrived to see the state he was in, horrified at what she saw.

David would succumb to his injuries three days later but not before his organs were harvested. His legacy of life now lives on in seven organ recipients.

David's lungs are now Lance Lewis' lungs. He wrote this on the last anniversary of David's death and wanted me to share it here:

Eleven years ago today, I awoke from a successful double lung transplant. Because of that transplant, I've had an additional 4,015 days with my wife, watched our children grow into amazing adults and parents, and enjoyed the birth of five additional grandchildren. However, my joy is tempered by the reality that my donor's family has spent the same 4,015 days without their son and brother.

At Jo and Spencer's request, I humbly, along with five other brothers in blue, carried David to his final resting place in Crown Hill Cemetery, where many other Indianapolis police officers killed in the line of duty rest.

David was a true warrior. If it could happen to him, it could happen to anyone of us. Does this help shed some light on why police officers find themselves on the defensive, always suspicious of those we encounter on the streets?

In November 2011, department positions were shuffled around, and I was named deputy chief of Operations to fill a vacancy created. I was asked to continue the progressive crime initiatives city-wide. My team and I identified the most violent areas for criminal activity throughout the city. I was asked by *The*

Star about my approach to targeting hot spots. "I said I want guns, I want dope, I want crimes of violence out of these areas," they quoted me as saying.[192] We saw results via aggressive and surgical policing targeting the most violent areas and offenders.

Within the first year of being deputy chief, I received a call from Julie, my son's mother, asking if I could come to her house. We had worked out our initial co-parenting bumps years earlier and now had a civil relationship. Matthew was at school, so I wasn't sure what the meeting was about. We sat on the front porch. Without much fanfare, she told me she had stage 4 breast cancer and the prognosis was not good. She was preparing to die. She knew Matthew would receive some of her death benefits, but with no living spouse, half of that money would be lost. Her plan, if I would agree to it, was that she and I marry before she died so that I could receive the surviving spouse benefits to help raise Matthew.

I was stunned.

I remember offering her platitudes, telling her she'd make it through, that she shouldn't be talking about dying. I honestly did not think she would die—at least not then. I told her I'd think about her plan, but I encouraged her to focus on her treatment and getting better. I left her house and went back to work, thinking the whole conversation was not something I'd have to deal with anytime soon. Matter of fact, I remember thinking, *Julie will outlive me. There's nothing to worry about.*

The stress and demands of that position were overwhelming for me at times, especially because I held myself accountable and took crime reduction to heart. Personnel issues, citizen complaints, and community requests seemed endless. There was no way to address everything. We had fewer officers on the department, and resources were scarce. At times, I felt like I was failing miserably. That job gave me a greater understanding of my former chief, Paul Annee. After my shooting, he too was trying to walk a fine line—a tight rope—searching for common ground between the necessities of policing, and the rights and dignity of those we are sworn to protect.

By then, my post work drinking was out of hand, and I knew it. I started missing calls in the middle of the night regarding my officers. On several occasions, I would wake up in the morning and learn that one of my guys had been involved in an officer-involved shooting the night before, or that one had been injured during a violent encounter. Late one night, I awoke to the phone ringing. One of my officers had been shot after responding to a domestic violence call. "It doesn't sound good, boss," they said on the phone. I was still intoxicated from the previous night. I couldn't risk driving. The troops needed to see me at the hospital as they watched another brother die. I failed them.

There were times in blackout that I would drive to the liquor store to buy more alcohol. I only knew this by finding the receipt and the empty bottle the next day. I often sent texts while blotto that were either extremely confrontational or made absolutely no sense at all. I forged the unfortunate habit of checking my phone as soon as I woke up to see what damage control needed to be done. On one particular morning, I called my downtown commander to check in with her on a few things. I started talking to her and was met with silence on the other end of the phone. She finally managed to say that while she knew I was her boss, she wasn't happy with the way I talked to her when I called her last night.

I was mortified.

With regret, I told her, "I have no recollection of talking to you last night. I was hammered. I don't remember what I said to you, but I'm sorry."

My chief and assistant chief of police at the time started putting two and two together. They didn't think I could effectively lead the Operations Division any longer. In February of 2014, I was demoted back to captain. Although I was assigned to North District, it only went south from there.

CHAPTER 9

SOLITUDE'S LAST DANCE

In the summer of 2014, I couldn't take it anymore. Losing the appointed rank of Deputy Chief was messing with my mind. I ruminated daily: did I let my troops down? Did I do enough? Suicidal ideation was a daily concern. It seemed my gun found its way into my mouth more than my toothbrush. I was scared that I might just kill myself.

It occurs to me today that part of what was happening was a withdrawal process from the adrenaline that came from holding a high-pressure position. My body was feeding me the intoxicating hormone on the daily as deputy chief. After going back to my permanent rank of Captain, I was showing up for work, but I was phoning it in. The shifts felt tedious and meaningless. Without fires to put out and chaos to handle, I wasn't sure what my purpose was for existing.

I knew I needed help.

I had been trying most of my life to cope on my own with an overwhelming storm of anger, anxiety, and depression. Like they say in Alcoholics Anonymous (AA), my best thinking got me here, and I feared I was about to crash and burn completely. I couldn't do it alone anymore.

I tried a suggested intensive outpatient program. But each day after treatment, I would leave at 5 p.m., go home to my empty condo and ruminate. Several weeks into the program, I was drinking again. In fact, I failed the urine test on the day I was supposed to graduate. I had been lying about drinking throughout the short-term program but dodged the urine test bullet up until then. Maybe I just wasn't ready for help. Certainly, I wasn't in a state that I could be trusted to leave treatment, go home alone every night, and not drink.

It was around that time that I had a pivotal conversation with a ranking captain on the force. Brian knew I needed help, and part of his job was to provide that for us. "Have you ever talked to anyone about PTSD?" he asked.

PTSD. A light turned on. I was certainly familiar with the term. But why had the thought that I might be struggling with it never crossed my mind? Maybe it was because I associated the term with an acute reaction that happens immediately after a traumatic event and then goes away. I didn't think it would be the problem all these years later. But I came to learn how my failure to address my mental and emotional state after the shooting probably led to the severity of my drinking and depression. In *The Art of Hypnotic Regression Therapy*, Bruce N. Eimer writes:

> As a clinical psychologist, I have treated many people over the years who suffered with PTSD. It has been my experience that if people suffering an acute reaction to the stress (i.e. soon after an extraordinary life-threatening event that has been

experienced either first hand or vicariously) receive early and appropriate intervention (e.g., critical incident stress counseling), they can often be saved years of severe distress and dysfunction. Unfortunately, in most cases, people who have experienced critical incidents do not receive the appropriate early intervention and their acute post-traumatic stress is often compounded by stressors emanating from supervisors, administrators, company policies, community and societal responses, the news media, relatives, neighbors, friends and so on (condemnation, negative publicity and judgements, shaming, shunning gossip, rejection, unreasonable administrative demands from superiors at work that either prescribe unhealthy changes or prohibit healthy changes, etc.) These stressors raise the PTSD survivor's anxiety levels and anxiety related symptoms such as hyper-vigilance, guilt, intrusive thoughts and images including flashbacks, nightmares, affective blunting, social withdrawal, activity avoidance and dissociation. These clusters of symptoms unabated can eventually lead to severe depression.

Over time, (typically months), a normal acute stress reaction evolves into an acute case of PTSD. At this point, it is still amenable to efficacious treatment. However, if not treated within this window, the PTSD is essentially a dissociative condition.[193]

After briefly discussing PTSD with that captain, he gave me the number of a doctor other department members used. When I called, the receptionist said they were booked solid and couldn't get me in for weeks. In a hopeless state of mind, I remember this response sounded like complete indifference rather than just a standard, reasonable reply from a practice that was at capacity.

In desperation, I conducted my own internet search for some-one —anyone—who might be able to help. I entered the keywords trauma, PTSD, and Jungian psychotherapy. Even three decades later, I was still drawn into Jung's theory of the shadow, or a person's dark side. A local psychotherapy group was one of only a few that came up. I went to their website and looked through the bios of the therapists in their group. Despite the fact that I was flailing in the darkness of full-blown alcoholism, I let my intuition be my guide.

I landed on a woman named Lisa whose profile said she worked with trauma and PTSD. I called and scheduled an appointment. I must have made the gravity of my situation clear to her, because she was able to get me in that week. I also searched for inpatient rehab programs that dealt with trauma and addiction. I found a place called The Ranch that was situated approximately an hour away from Nashville, TN.

A few days later, I drove to Lisa's office incredibly hung-over from the night before. I'm not one to easily spill my guts, but it was as if a damn had broken from the sheer pressure of the emotional chaos I'd been holding inside. There, for the first time in years, I opened up. I told her that I had killed a man in the line of duty nearly three decades before. I had hurt others as well during violent on-duty encounters. I didn't understand how to process all of that—after nearly 25 years of pushing it down.

I told her I knew I was an alcoholic. I was consuming a fifth or more of vodka every day. And I had recently lost an appointed rank, more than likely because of it. I informed her that my son's mother was dying of cancer and I was in the process of accepting the fact that I was about to become a single parent. I also mentioned I was currently in a tumultuous and failing relationship with a woman I loved and hated at the same time. Looking back now, I think it was in that moment the thought occurred to me that I was the common denominator in all of all my failed relationships. And there were many—friends, lovers, and colleagues. In less than an hour, I had convinced her that I was too fucked up for a standard talk therapy scenario.

I wanted to know—how did I go from wanting to help others to the person now sitting before her?

"Can you help me? Please," I begged her in tears.

She encouraged me to admit myself to an inpatient rehab program, and soon. If I chose not to do inpatient, she said she would need to see me at least three times a week if we were to have a shot at sorting things out. I left still in tears and feeling utterly hopeless. I remember pleading again right before I left, "Can you help me?" She tried to calmly assure me that she could, but I sensed that even she wasn't sure if I'd make it.

I met my mom for lunch the next day. For the first time, I admitted to her just how bad of shape I was in. I tried to summarize what I'd been dealing with internally for the last 25 years, and how much my alcoholism had escalated. She was stunned. She said she had no idea I'd been struggling that severely or drinking that much. "I was watching Dr. Phil the other day," she said, "and they mentioned this rehab place called The Ranch." I'm not sure if it was the same place or not, but I took it as a sign. It was settled then, she said. The woman who gave birth to me 51 years ago was ready to write a check to give me yet another chance at life.

Lisa called me that afternoon just like she said she would to check on me. I told her my plan. She seemed relieved. We agreed to check back in with each other when I returned.

I spoke with our department administrators and we came up with a plan for me to take a leave of absence from my job.

And just like that, I was off.

The Ranch—Tour I

Some were concerned, my mom especially, that I planned to drive there myself. "You don't need any more problems," she warned. "Take a bus or fly, but don't drive yourself."

I thought about it. "I'll be fine," I convinced her. I wanted my own car with me as a way out if I got desperate.

But even more than that, I wanted to hang out with a bottle one last time. Like most addicts and alcoholics know, the task in front of me felt overwhelmingly daunting. I was saying goodbye to that old friend who always had my back through the pain, anxiety, depression, and fear, or so I had convinced myself.

Before leaving Indianapolis, I searched for a motel near The Ranch and made reservations so I could enjoy one more night in isolation before sobering up. I left the day before I was to report and headed south. I ruminated on the wreck my life had become as I drove.

A sober life. The thought was frightening. Ego convinced me of that.

I thought, what in the hell would a sober life even look like? I had been mired in addiction for so long I didn't know who I was anymore. My true self no longer existed. At least, the connection had been severed. I didn't make it three hours into my trip before I stopped to get a bite to eat. I had a cocktail and chips at the bar to calm my nerves and mind, which was still navigating the fog from hitting it the night before. I continued my journey to the motel. I bought a couple bottles of wine at a nearby store and locked myself in my room. I just wanted to be alone.

That place called Solitude, which I referenced in my suicidal poem. Away from people and fear, as lonely as it is, still felt like home.

I watched a movie and savored both bottles of wine. I tried to make them last as best as an alcoholic can. I would be on that sober train starting the next day. I tried to enjoy it as I lost myself in TV and my cell phone. I knew I would be forfeiting my phone the next day at rehab. It was protocol at The Ranch.

I was supposed to report at noon for processing at the administrative office. I remember getting there around 11:00 a.m. I talked myself out of driving away several times. No part of me wanted to be there or face the weaknesses that brought me to this point in my life. At noon, I willed myself out of my car and checked in. There, I was given a packet, including the short but poignant book written by Don Miguel Ruiz, *The Four Agreements: A Practical Guide to Personal Freedom.*

After checking in, I was escorted a short distance to Piney Lodge. It sounds rustic, but it was nothing more than a small block medical facility that housed clients through the withdrawal process. There, my belongings were searched, and items confiscated. They wanted to make sure I didn't have any contraband on my person or in my luggage. "Can't have these," the attendant said. The shampoo and mouthwash I brought with me had a trace of alcohol in it.

"Seriously? You think I'm gonna drink that shit," I asked.

"Oh, it's happened before," he said.

I thought, *Am I in rehab or prison?*

I remained at Piney Lodge for nearly a week under medical supervision along with other addicts—heroin, meth, opiates, sex addicts—you name it. I remember being in a small common room my first day. Some guy introduced himself and asked what brought me to The Ranch.

As we were shaking hands, I replied, "I'm Scott, and I'm an alcoholic. What brings you here?"

"I jack off too much I'm told," he replied.

I didn't ask that question again in the future, nor did I shake any other clients' hands.

Those first few days, I sat by myself in the day room and read *The Four Agreements*. It offered a simple Toltec code of personal conduct, if you will, to guide one's behavior and liberation from self-limiting beliefs. The agreements seem so easy, but many addicts fail at all four. They are:

1. Be impeccable with your word. (Addicts are a deceptive lot.)
2. Don't take anything personally. (Addicts usually do, which gives them yet another reason to self-medicate and take things personally again.)
3. Don't make assumptions. (Addicts often assume the worst in every situation.)
4. Always do your best. (None of us got here on a winning streak.)

I vowed to put these simple agreements to work in my daily life.

After the supervised withdrawal period, I was assigned to a house. There, I would meet the ten guys I'd spend the next three weeks with. I soon learned I had much more in common with heroin addicts and other junkies than I ever could have imagined. I thought I was somehow set apart from these groups of people. I realized how I'd let my profession make me judgmental.

We had daily group therapy with the house counselors, attended educational classes, and had weekend outings off-campus, such as visiting Nashville. We were also required to attend group support meetings, whether it be AA, Narcotics Anonymous (NA), or the Buddhist Refuge Recovery program. I was also assigned a personal trauma therapist. She diagnosed me for the first time with PTSD. What I assumed would be an acute period morphed into a chronic condition, and I had been drinking so regularly, it happened without me even noticing or understanding it. My therapist also said I was an Adult Child of an Alcoholic (ACA), which came with its own set of symptoms that I needed to work through. In fact, she said the ACA issues probably had more deleterious effects on me than the trauma of the shooting.

And to think I showed up at The Ranch's doorstep just an alcoholic.

Shortly after that diagnosis, I learned via a letter from home that one of my officers on TAC shift had been killed in the line of duty. Officer Perry Renn and others responded to a call in a neighborhood where people heard shots being fired on Saturday, July 5, 2014. *The Star* reported that upon arriving at the scene, the officers approached a group of individuals standing around a nearby alley. That's when the suspect pulled an assault rifle and exchanged gunfire with the officers for several minutes. Renn was injured and later transported to the hospital in critical condition.[194] He didn't make it. A member of the suspect's family would later infer it was somehow Renn's fault for getting out of his patrol car. After his death, Perry's widow, Lynn, helped initiate the "I Will Always Get Out of my Car" campaign, a statement that would be emblazoned on local t-shirts. The slogan caught on and became a nationwide pledge by police officers.

I discussed the impact Perry's murder had on me in one-on-one therapy sessions. Again, I felt I had failed as a byproduct of my addiction. I should have been there for Perry and the rest of my troops, but instead I was sitting in rehab. I couldn't even attend his funeral in his honor. Another reason to feel deep shame.

During sessions, I would also talk about my shooting, the court drama, and the violent encounters I'd had on the job. I was exposed to a technique called Eye Movement Desensitization and Reprocessing (EMDR). It seemed to help a great deal to release the fear and anxiety that had been trapped at a subconscious and cellular level.

I came back from The Ranch after 28 days and felt great. I was on the proverbial pink cloud they talk about in recovery circles, when the addict is newly clean and sober and feels incredibly positive about sobriety and life in general. Once back in Indianapolis, things were going much smoother, or so I thought.

I soon found out Julie was in the hospital, and it didn't look good. The cancer was aggressive, and it was clear she wouldn't hold on much longer. I started seeing Lisa again a couple times a week to help me cope. I was broken-hearted for my son. He was eight years old. And I was about to become a single parent, so we spent a good deal of time focusing on how I could manage my son, my recovery, and maintain my sobriety. In the first few weeks out of rehab, I was stabilizing and slowly getting my footing.

Then one day, I got the phone call I'd been dreading because it meant I had to make a difficult decision. Julie was being transitioned from the hospital into home hospice care. If I wanted to marry her and secure her pension for Matthew, like she had offered when she told me about her diagnosis, I needed to make that decision now. "It's for your son," several close friends and mentors advised me.

One night, Matthew and I were sitting on the couch watching one of his favorite movies for the hundredth time. I noticed he was tuned out. He had a pensive look on his face.

I said, "What's wrong, little buddy?"

He turned to me and said, "Dad, is my mom going to live?"

I paused, caught off guard by the question.

"Tell me the truth," he said.

Somberly, I shook my head. I said, "No, buddy, she's not."

He ran to his room and shut the door. I checked on him, but in tears he said, "I just want to be alone."

In the end, I listened to the people still in my life who I trusted, because I couldn't think through it clearly by myself. On the advice of my friends and my therapist, I decided to go through with the wedding ceremony, but I still never felt sure I was doing the right thing. I went to an AA meeting after. When it was my turn to share, I said, "If... If I can just make it until midnight, I will have been sober for two months."

I didn't make it until midnight.

That night I drove to the liquor store and bought a bottle. Glass in hand, I was listening to my "drinking and thinking" playlist again.

I continued to take my son to school and pick him up. I would, in anguish, take him back to Julie's house every afternoon so he could watch his mother die a little bit more each day. It tore me apart. Only a few days after the marriage, she was gone. Matthew stayed with his older brother and Julie's family while they grieved together and planned the funeral.

I wrestled with the marriage vows I'd taken. Ruminating. It wasn't long before my mind wandered back to the solution that I'd danced with for so many years. I had pushed it down for the past few months, but the alcohol brought it back. In that dark head space once again, it seemed clear what I needed to do.

My ability to think rationally was compromised. In my head, I was marrying a dying woman for money. Consumed with guilt and shame, I finally resolved to commit suicide.

I formulated my plan the next morning. I met with Madi in the early afternoon so I could see her one last time. We decided to meet at a Starbucks. We sat there for an hour or so, not saying much to each other. My daughter talks about as much as I do, especially when it comes to feelings. She didn't know it at the time, but I was trying to say goodbye. I was leaving my little partner—the eyes of chance—that rode with me every night there on the dash of my police car.

The pain was unbearable, but my thoughts seemed lucid. *Today*, I thought. *Today.*

My plan was to leave Starbucks, head directly to the liquor store, buy a handle of vodka, get peacefully drunk, and then blow my brains out later that evening. I was finally comfortable and eerily at peace with my decision. The world will be better off without me, I convinced myself. My son would be better off as well, I thought, despite the fact that cancer had just claimed his mother's life. I couldn't see how illogical and unreasonable those thoughts were. They made perfect sense at the time. I was ready to go. I think Madi was intuitively worried about me, but I lied and convinced her I was fine. I told her I needed to leave because I wanted to go to an AA meeting that started soon. She said she thought that was a good idea. We said goodbye and parted ways.

I immediately bought the vodka as planned. I went home and started drinking. At some point, I must have called Mary, a friend from AA. I don't remember what I said to her, but she sensed I was drunk and in trouble. I asked her to come over, but she couldn't at that time. She must have asked me if she could call someone to help me. I gave her Tammy's number.

Tammy remembers she was out buying books when she got a call from a woman she didn't know. "It was strange," she said, "because she called me 'Tam' and only people I know call me that." Mary told her I was suicidal. Tammy agreed to go and check on me. She arrived around 7 p.m. I was incredibly drunk and depressed. I just cried as she sat with me. We both talked with Mary on the phone, and I agreed to give Tammy the Glock .45 pistol I had ready.

I unloaded it and handed it to her. She took it outside and locked it in her car.

Tammy said my darkness only worsened as time went on. We sat there on my couch the rest of the night as I drained the vodka bottle. I wanted more. She said I was talking somewhat incoherently about papers I was supposed to sign the next day for Julie. I was referring to the death certificate. Her surviving spouse now, I was the one required to sign the document.

I was very drunk and finally got tired, emotionally and physically drained from crying, and decided to lie down. Tammy lay there next to me to ensure that I passed out. After I did, she fell asleep too.

I woke up early the next morning. She was still asleep. I was still intoxicated. I quietly got up so she wouldn't hear me. I immediately found her purse, grabbed her car keys, and snuck outside to her car. There, I grabbed my pistol, reloaded it, and went back upstairs. I was sitting on the couch with the gun on my lap when she woke up. She said later, "I thought I hid my keys from you so you wouldn't find them. I felt like a failure, because all I was supposed to do was get the weapon and make sure you no longer had access to it." I started searching my cabinets for any kind of liquor I could find. I found a full bottle of Pernod, an anise-flavored liqueur. As an avid cook, I happened to have it on hand. I started drinking it straight out of the bottle. The liquorish scent was overwhelming as I forced it down. (That smell will forever take me back to this moment.)

Tammy continued to try and talk me out of it. I had already made my mind up. I kept asking her to leave because I didn't want her to watch me do it. She kept asking if there was someone we could call that might be able to help. She was trying to anchor me to this life by bringing up my kids and how it would affect them.

She said as the alcohol kicked in, I relaxed and was off-guard. She was able to put her shoes on and secure her car keys without me noticing. I briefly laid the gun down on the couch. In that split second, she grabbed it and headed for the door. She ran down the stairs and dropped the magazine and the one in the chamber. I chased after her but couldn't keep up in my state. She ran to her car and locked the pistol inside, then immediately called 911. I knew she was on the phone with them. I ran back to my condo but didn't have my keys to unlock the entry door. I pushed all the buttons, hoping that someone would buzz me in. A neighbor was coming out at the time. "Hey buddy," he said to me as I ran right past him and back upstairs, locking myself inside.

The police eventually showed up. Though Tammy had taken the weapon I'd planned to use, everyone on the scene was well aware that I had several other firearms in my home. Sergeant Jo Moore, David's mother, was the first supervisor to arrive on scene. I was on the phone with Tammy, so she handed Jo the phone. She tried to talk some sense into me, but I wasn't listening. "I even tried a little guilt trip. I tried to talk to you about David," she said.

Soon, more officers showed up. Tammy told them what had been going on. The former wife of a SWAT guy, she knew what came next—vehicles, snipers, media. She repeatedly begged them not to call SWAT. She was trying to protect me from having a team that I once ran come to the scene and apprehend me.

The way Tammy described it, the SWAT call-up happened, and it was typical—countless vehicles, SWAT van, ambulance, a helicopter, and the Red Cross wagon. The crew wasn't communicating with Tammy about what was going on, and they took her phone in case I tried to call. All they would tell her was, "Scotty's ok, and he's talking to us." This went on for most of the day. I have no recollection of being on the phone with them. Jo remembers me saying to her, "Don't let anyone come through that door. I don't want to be responsible for anyone getting hurt." I was at least coherent enough to know I didn't want to force one of my own guy's hand into a suicide by police situation. She said they all took me at my word and decided they wouldn't force entry. "I was uncomfortable sitting in that van and talking to you in a SWAT situation, because, well… you wrote the book," Jo admitted all these years later.

Danny Overley came to the scene, the man who'd been like a father to me throughout my policing career, but the guys wouldn't let him talk to me for fear that I was waiting on him to say goodbye. "I wanted to be able to talk to you," he told me. "We'd been through the worst I've ever seen a person. And how you were so resilient to get back up. What I wanted to say to you was, 'This really looks bad for you now. But look at other officers who've been through this. You can get to the other side of this.'"

At some point, Lisa, my therapist, showed up to assist. I must have given someone her number. I talked with her on the phone several times but don't remember any of it. Since I was no longer in possession of my pistol, I tried loading one of my other weapons, but in my drunken state, I couldn't find the right ammunition. I gave up and decided to try and slice my wrist. I found my biggest, sharpest butcher knife. I cut into my left wrist as I spoke on the phone with various people—no recollection of who. When I thought I had cut deep enough and blood starting spewing, I would lay back and wait for the end. But then the bleeding would stop, so I tried a few more times to no end.

Eventually, the alcohol wore off and I became more lucid. A former SWAT brother finally convinced me to come out and to go back into rehab. (Thanks, Ted.)

I surrendered to my former teammates—the guys I once led. I was put in the back of a police car under immediate detention.

Now that's a bad day.

Madi, whose sense of humor is about as sick as mine, was allowed to come up to the car at my request. When she saw the blood all over my sleeves, she asked, "You been painting, Dad?" Tammy stayed around to sign documents after the police searched my condo. She cleaned up the blood on the walls and packed some clothes for me.

I was off to my second tour at The Ranch.

CHAPTER 10

THE SHADOW OF THE BADGE

This time I flew.

I was under suicide watch, so there was no way anyone would let me drive to Tennessee again. I was taken to the airport. Representatives from The Ranch were waiting for me. Looking back, this go-around in rehab was much harder than the first. I was swimming in the haunting memories and thoughts of my failed suicide attempt and the mess that came with it. All the pieces of the event replayed incessantly in my head—the involvement of my ex-wife, my daughter, my team. And another thought kept circling.

You couldn't even succeed at killing yourself.

The gravity of what I had gone through in the weeks following my first stay at The Ranch produced an oppressive, seemingly intolerable mental state. Not believing it was possible, I was in an even darker headspace this time.

I was assigned to Creek House and had two new house therapists and a new trauma therapist. My initial meeting with my primary therapist, Charlie, rattled me even further. After I sat across from him at his desk, he told me he had reviewed my psycho-social notes from my first stay. He said, "Tell me more about the shooting."

Here we go again, I thought. I was so sick and tired of telling my story.

After I finished talking, Charlie said our first therapy objective was for me to address or accept what might be my racist undertones. I almost walked out on him, which is my go-to reaction in those situations, but I'm glad I didn't.

Later that evening, I sat with Charlie's words and tried to put the puzzle pieces together. What was really going on with me here? Was I, in fact, a racist? I started searching the past and journaling some thoughts. I had a completely white upbringing. I attended nearly all-white schools. My dad prided himself on our German heritage. I shot a Black man during Black Expo. Then I thought about the barrage of community messages I had received throughout my career. The media, the Concerned Clergy, Jesse Jackson— hadn't they all been saying the thing that Charlie was asking me to confront? I thought about the catch phrases: "shoot a Black, get a plaque" (the statement used to mock the award I received after the shooting), "controversial cop." I thought about the casket that was carried in protest at the City-County Building. I remembered the guy who approached me at the gun show.

Maybe I did have an underlying sense of privilege that I had been unaware of previously. But I also knew there was more to the story. There was another side to this balance sheet. I had been lauded for progressive crime reduction strategies. I worked hard to give second chances to minorities who might have otherwise spent decades in prison. I had risked my personal safety countless times to protect and defend just as many Black victims as any other race.

I realized that three decades later, I had never done this work. I never took a hard look at myself as a police officer from the perspective of both camps. It was easy for me to anchor on the negative things people said about me. I soaked them up like a sponge then used them as a reason to drink. Sitting there in Nashville, I had to come to terms with the fact that there was truth to be found in both camps. Those who called me a cold-blooded killer and those who called me a hero. They were both right. There is both light and dark in all of us.

The next day, I was exposed to psychodrama. This is a technique used by therapists to assist clients in revisiting past traumatic experiences through guided scenarios and role playing in a group setting. I participated in several during this tour.

During one session, a couple of my house buddies were asked to play the roles of Julie when she was still alive, and a current girlfriend. The house therapists were like some sort of version of "good cop, bad cop." One would talk to me calmly and rationally as he coached me to tell Julie and my girlfriend what I really thought and felt about them. The other gave me a whiffle bat and commanded me to hit a pillow to channel my anger.

I wasn't entirely comfortable with this scenario. It felt forced, and I was self-conscious. I've never been good at role playing or acting. But I was in no position to resist the treatment the addiction experts were prescribing for me. My best thinking landed me back in rehab. I wanted to get better, so I participated. I said a few things to each of them, trying to summon up the anger I felt.

When Randy, the bad cop, didn't feel enough emotion was coming out of me, he taunted me. "Hit it harder," he'd say. The goal was to provoke my anger enough to unearth my emotions, address them, and heal them.

I hit the pillow harder. I tried to pretend these grown men were grown women as I told them how I felt about them. Apparently, I still wasn't worked up enough for Randy's liking.

"You call that hitting? I thought you were a big tough guy. You want me to show you how to use a bat like a man?"

Suddenly, a switch flipped. The rage and anger flooded me. I threw the bat down, turned to face Randy and walked toward him.

"No, I don't **fucking** need you to show me how to use a **fucking** bat!"

Charlie, the good cop, stepped in front of me as I watched Randy back away, eyes wide with fear. The guys in the group were on their feet now. Cole, one of my closest friends from The Ranch, hightailed it out of the room, not one who liked to be around confrontation. Cole told me later, "I thought you were about to kill him."

The therapists decided this was a good place to break. Charlie told me to go get some fresh air. Outside at a picnic table, I sat alone, trying to collect myself. Another friend from the group, John, approached me and sat next to me.

"We saw the beast, bro," he said.

I stared straight ahead. I didn't want to look at him. I knew all too well what he was saying.

"Yeah, I know." I was fighting back tears, but I was losing.

"Dude," he said, "you gotta let that shit go."

I let the tears come freely now. I trusted John so I let myself sit there with him and cry.

"That's the person I hate," I said. I knew who John had seen. I knew exactly who the Beast was. He could be triggered by someone putting their hands on me on the street just as easily as he could be triggered by alcohol.

Charlie and I sat down together later to process what happened in group. He said he saw a "murderous rage" in my eyes when I turned toward Randy.

My journal entry from that day reads:

"I'm here to come to accept the part of me that can kill without remorse—who might be racist, who can hurt people physically and emotionally—and let him go metaphorically, as I'm afraid that part will always be a part of me, after a lifetime's worth of feeding the Beast, it's now time to tame it."

Here's what I came to accept as my truth as I reflected on my career. Sometimes, I was the good guy. I sincerely wanted to help. It's why I pursued the profession. I wanted to be the knight in shining armor for my community. But there were times, maybe after I had seen one too many bad guys do one too many bad things, when I would snap and become someone I didn't recognize. I said and did things out of emotion, all in the name of apprehending people I had generically labeled as criminals, thugs, shit-birds, crooks, perps, gangbangers, junkies, drunks, or just all-around assholes. If you can label one, or a group, as the evil other, you can easily justify your actions against them. There was little time for empathetic consideration of what that individual might be going through in his or her personal life that might warrant their behavior.

Another member of The Ranch staff I had the pleasure of meeting was Daniel, a member of the Oglala Lakota tribe. He is one of those old, venerable souls who, when he walks into a room, gives you the feeling he communes with those from a different existential plane. I had the honor of participating in a Lakota sweat lodge ceremony under his tutelage.

I had never experienced anything numinous until this ceremony. As we sat in a circle in the dark, heated tent, Daniel chanted, sang spiritual songs and played a drum. We took turns sharing with the members of the circle something we needed to unburden ourselves of—something we had carried for too long, or something bothering us—that we could now release within the safety of the lodge. Daniel taught us to finish our share with the phrase, "All My Relations," which is a short, simple Lokata prayer recognizing and honoring the interconnectedness of all beings on the planet, including the animals and insects.

As each person spoke and finished with, "All my relations," I noticed an incredible feeling of connectedness with that person. I felt their joy and their pain. It reinforced for me the idea that we truly are all one. Daniel had shown me that maybe there was a light at the end of my dark-night tunnel.

When I returned, my son came to live with me full-time. I immediately restarted therapy with Lisa. I was encouraged to attend meetings and get a sponsor. Lisa knew a man she thought might be able to help me. She knew I wasn't a fan of 12-step meetings, nor organized religion, but she recommended a rabbi who had many years of recovery because we had many common interests, oddly enough. As he and I began to meet regularly and walk through the steps together, I told him I was apprehensive about the fourth step: a searching and fearless moral inventory of ourselves. He gave me a simple guideline to follow. List your regrets and your resentments and be honest. It's that simple. He said I would feel better after I did that and shared it with him.

I wrote out my lists of those I'd harmed and those I resented for various reasons. At first, I didn't think my list would be very long. It took me several weeks to compile, and when it was complete, the list filled the better part of a spiral notebook. I had no idea how much pent-up anger, resentment, and shameful regrets I compiled over the years.

I made arrangements to meet with my new sponsor and share my assignment. He could tell by the look on my face I was anxious. He said, "Don't worry, Scott, I've heard it all." That gave me some courage. With a deep breath, I started at the top of the list with the resentments: Leonard Barnett. I killed an unarmed Black man, I told him. Next on my list were the Rev. Jesse Jackson, Mayor Hudnutt, Chief Annee, and the Concerned Clergy. Tammy was on there as well. I resented her for having prevented my suicide. I looked up from my notebook to catch the stunned expression on my sponsor's face.

"So, let me get this straight. You resent your ex-wife for literally saving your life?"

I replied succinctly, "Yes." (Looking back now, of course I'm grateful. If it weren't for Tammy, I wouldn't be here today. Thank you, Tam.)

After several hours, I finished purging my soul and closed my notebook. My sponsor collected his thoughts, then said, "At this point, I usually tell my sponsees there's nothing you've told me that I haven't done myself or heard before, but with you, that's just not the case." Having taken comfort in the statement he made just a few hours ago, that nothing I said could shock him, his words hit me in the gut. I thought, *Wow. He's been sponsoring guys for over 20 years. I must really be a piece of shit.*

Lisa also encouraged me to attend a weekly group that her colleague was starting. It was designed for people with addiction and relationship problems. *Check and check,* I thought. The group began in January of 2015. It's clear that group was the genesis of building the sober and stable life I have today. But as is the case with many people who go through personal tragedy, it would get worse before it got better.

On day one of group therapy, I was the first to arrive. I sat alone in the room, anxiously waiting for the other new members. The first to walk in was a girl I'd never met or seen before. She sat across from me on the other side of the room, so we were directly facing each other. We were the only two in the room for the next several minutes before other members started arriving. We both remember—it wasn't awkward at all. Through conversation, an immediate connection was made. It was as if we had already known each other on some level.

That was Katy, who is now my wife.

I continued seeing Lisa twice a week while attending the group. A few months in, I found out the department was granting me a medical pension for PTSD, so I wouldn't be returning to work.

I was officially retired. Not sure how to handle life without my job, I started drinking again. It wasn't quite as all-consuming as before, but a few nights a week, after my son went to bed, I was hitting the bottle. At that point, I was still able to hide it from most people in my life, but Lisa figured it out very quickly when I started sending her drunken texts.

Things started getting even worse.

Our relationship changed from patient/client into something far less professional. With this in mind, she said we could no longer work together. She convinced me that I still needed to be in treatment and set me up with a colleague and friend of hers.

My first session with the new therapist started with us coming to an agreement on a lie I could tell others about why I left Lisa. "Let's talk about the elephant in the room," she said. Together, we came up with a story. I knew the question was inevitable after I had told so many how helpful Lisa had been in my initial recovery. I believed that she and The Ranch helped save my life. I knew my family, my sponsor, and my group therapist would want to know why I was switching. We decided that I would say I needed a therapist who had a more in-depth understanding of addiction to take me further in my recovery. The recovery community will tell you that lies keep you mired in shame and addiction. I was living one again.

I continued group therapy. The process of talking with others who understood addiction was healing. However, I also had my low moments in that room. One night, as one of the other members was sharing about the terrible things her alcoholism had caused her to do, she said, "Well, at least I can say I've never killed anyone."

Silence fell over the room. I finally said, "Unfortunately, I can't say that about myself."

Thou shalt not kill.

I thought of Tom Black, my friend and former co-worker who I'd had a few conversations with recently about policing and addiction. As a life-long agnostic, I never had to answer to any church for my actions. But Tom, who was raised in a strict Catholic family, was involved in a police-action shooting in 1989. The suspect, who had stolen a taxi, was ultimately shot and killed by Tom and other officers as they tried to apprehend him. As he recalled his struggles with the event all these years later, he gave me his take on killing a man:

> "I followed the edicts of the Catholic Church for the most part. After the shooting, at first I felt good because it was a bad guy. But there's a dark side to doing those things. The homicide guys told us, tactically, we did a great job. That felt really good. But then I remember crying the whole night. I went to therapy. Talked about what I did. Then it was a year later that I went to confession. It was a crusty old priest. I told him what happened. He goes, "Eh, that's not a sin! That's allowed. It's not murder. You were protecting yourself and your fellow officers." Basically, he told me it was that guy's choice. And the thing was—that freed me. That took that burden off of me—the "Thou Shalt Not Kill." Tactically, we were sound. We did everything we were supposed to do. But that church side of things played on me for a long time until I met with that priest."

I asked him, "What were your outlets for dealing with the emotions?"

"This bottle, that bottle," Tom said. "Depression kind of set in. I didn't have people to talk to. We didn't really talk about it. We would just get together and drink. It was always the job that kept me going. Just get back to work and hammer through. It was the one place I had control and I knew what I was doing."

Katy and I continued to really connect with each other in group. When she spoke, I was usually the first to offer her feedback and words of support, and vice versa. It was clear that we both felt very low about ourselves, but in each other, we were able to see all the wonderful things we were blind to in ourselves, despite the fact that in that group room, we were all privy to what we felt were the absolute worst things about ourselves. In other words, I knew all of her shit, and she knew all of mine. How many relationships start out that way? But still, she saw only my good, and I saw only hers. It was a connection unlike either of us had ever had.

Eventually Katy and I broke a major rule of group therapy guidelines—we exchanged numbers. We met for coffee and conversation a few times, but nothing more. She dropped out of group before its anticipated conclusion date, and we didn't talk much for several weeks. Then out of the blue, she texted me in December and asked if I wanted to meet for lunch. A few days later, we were sitting across from each other again at a restaurant, laughing, catching up, and listening to what we'd been struggling with since we'd last seen each other. It was clear we'd reconnected and that our bond was stronger than ever.

Christmas was the following week, and we both talked about how our plans were to stay home—alone. Back then, I couldn't recall a Christmas without alcohol involved. In the halls of AA, I often heard, "An alcoholic alone is in bad company." Katy had a good amount of clean time at that point and wanted to keep it that way, so she decided to stay away from family gatherings and parties. And I needed to avoid isolation. We made plans to get out of our houses and see a movie together on Christmas day. When we hugged goodbye that night after the movie, it was clear to me—this was the start of something.

Unfortunately, I still had my share of hard times ahead before I reached sobriety. I was still drinking and trying to hide it from everyone, including Katy. The new therapist was helping me sort things out, but I obviously wasn't ready to be honest and give up the bottle for good. I remember her cautioning me about moving into another relationship too quickly, especially with someone also in recovery. She said, "If your addict ever hooks up with her addict, you're both screwed." I decided not to heed her advice, and eventually, I stopped seeing that therapist all together. After my experience with Lisa, and then the lie I had to come up with in order to continue treatment, I lost faith in the local psychotherapeutic community altogether. With all the treatment I'd had in the last two years, why wasn't I staying sober? I figured, these therapists can't cure me, so who needs them?

Katy and I got more serious, and she eventually found out about the drinking. She stuck by me and took me to meetings, trying to help me find my balance. Then in June, she unexpectedly lost her mother. They'd had a very close relationship, and when she got back to Indianapolis after the funeral, her grief got the better of her. She started drinking along with me, though alcohol was never her drug of choice. For a brief period of time, our addicts met. And just as the therapist predicted—we were screwed.

That initial bout of drinking was short-lived. I would become angry and emotional when I drank too much, and it frightened Katy. We decided we needed to get our shit together. After several months of sobriety, we drove to the Outer Banks and eloped. As we sat at a crowded restaurant later that night, we struck up a conversation with a fellow vacationer sitting across from us. When we told him and his wife we'd just gotten married, he had two glasses of expensive champagne sent to us. And we were off again.

We convinced ourselves that we could handle a drink together every now and then, but a glass of wine here and there turned into a bottle or three. And now and again turned into every night. Soon, I was back to getting blackout drunk while Katy tried to manage the chaos that was unfolding as a result. Things went downhill again from there. Sometimes, we'd go for days without drinking, focusing on exercising, eating healthy, building our relationship, and attending meetings. But then one of us would have a bad day, giving us the perfect opportunity to convince ourselves that we deserved to have a few drinks that night to take the edge off and relax.

This continued for months—going back and forth between sobriety and drinking. One day, after we had managed to put together a long stretch of sobriety, I met my mom for lunch. I was feeling great that day. I was clear-headed. Katy and I had been eating healthy and working out. We were completely in love and were feeling optimistic about the future. My mom asked me how

I was doing, and I remember telling her, "This is the happiest I've ever been." I planned on cooking my special chicken wings for us that night for dinner. Matthew was staying the night with his brother. The plan was to chill and watch some Netflix. I decided it was a good night to have a few drinks—why not? What could it hurt? (Turns out binge watching Sons of Anarchy while drunk was not optimal for my psyche.)

How can you go from being completely happy one minute, and 12 hours later, wake up to find yourself in jail?

I drank too much. I crossed the line into blackout that night. While checking my phone, I saw a text from a family member that triggered my rage. I decided I was going to text her back and give her a piece of my mind. Katy tried to talk me out of it because I was too drunk. That's when I turned on her. Suddenly, she was the enemy. I became angry and violent. Not knowing what I was doing, or even who she was (she says I was calling her the wrong name), I attacked her. A neighbor heard her screams and called the police. They came quickly. I woke up in jail with absolutely no recollection of what happened the night before.

Looking back now, I'm reminded of the words of William Alexander, the reporter from the *Recorder* who said of me in 1990, "Mark my words, this kid will get jammed up again, and soon." It wasn't soon. It was three decades later, after having spent most of my career trying to make myself, and my community, better. What I failed to do was address the underlying trauma that I had stuffed down for so long.

Fitz came to bail me out. The police had issued a standard no contact order between Katy and me, so I couldn't go home. She was making plans to stay with her family while we figured out our next steps, so I went to stay with my mom. Matthew was staying with his brother. Someone, most likely a relative of Julie's, called Child Protective Services (CPS). Once they became involved, we temporarily lost custody of him. A new hell started to unfold for us as we surveyed the damage and tried to put the pieces back together.

Katy and I started working both with individual therapists and with a couple's therapist to try and course correct. We had a long road ahead of us if we wanted to be reunited as a family. I once again entered treatment—this time as an outpatient at a local facility. There were several goals we both needed to achieve before we could regain custody of Matthew and move forward. It was an incredibly difficult time for all three of us. Supervised visitations, drug tests, family therapy, and support meetings filled our calendars over the next several weeks.

Finally, we won the battle. The family judge overseeing our case looked at all the steps we'd taken. She said to me, "I talked to Matthew one on one. He told me you're a great dad when you're not drinking." She made the decision to reunite us. The transition was difficult, but we continued to attend family therapy to help us find equilibrium after all we'd been through. Katy and I had been talking about moving since we'd been together. After I shared my dream with her of living on the Outer Banks after retirement, she made it her mission to make it happen.

We made it to our new home in July of 2018. Back in Indianapolis, Katy and I both gravitated to SMART Recovery meetings, a secular alternative to 12-step groups. We found the program immensely helpful, so much so that we started the first

SMART Recovery meeting on the Outer Banks. After the path I've walked, I want to pay it forward and help others who have been on a similar journey of trauma and addiction. In fact, some of the first members who came to our meeting are war veterans who deal with PTSD. I try and offer feedback and guidance based on the years I spent navigating my prolonged dark night of the soul. I also spent a year as a domestic violence crisis line operator for our community—something I did to make an amends.

My life today looks completely different than it did four years ago. We live a mostly drama-free existence here on the island, filled with weekly trips to the beach, writing projects that we take on together, and raising our now 17-year-old son, who Katy took on as her own. We still have struggles, but they're the same everyday struggles we all have.

After having stored away the trauma of the past 32 years of my life for so long, I'm working on unpacking it—looking at its implications on a personal level, but also on a more global level. The first step to help in healing others is healing yourself.

CHAPTER 11

PEACE BEGINS WITHIN

I n 2017, I began tearing through those boxes of newspaper clippings from my mom. I talked to some of the people involved. I
relived, cried, raged, and ruminated. And today, as I try to finally
put some closure to this chapter of my life that has remained open
for the last 32 years, I still find myself asking questions. Some are
painful and unanswerable but need to be examined.

First, I wonder if and how things could have turned out differently if the players in the Leonard Barnett case had made different
choices. Barnett could have chosen not to hold up the Taco Bell.
Having robbed the business, he could have chosen to pull over
peacefully and submit to a lawful arrest. He didn't. What was going
on in his world that drove him from the son Len that everyone
knew and loved to a violent, armed felon? We'll never know, but I
wish now, more than ever, I could ask him.

I could have chosen to remain at White Castle, finish my cup
of coffee, and not get involved. I didn't. That wasn't the training
I received, the instinct in my gut, or the decision on my heart. I
could have, as plaintiff's attorney Richard Waples suggested, not
left the cover of my vehicle, taking up a more tactical position by

waiting for backup and not advancing on Barnett. I didn't. Once he chose not to surrender and I chose to pull the trigger, our fates were sealed.

What could the police administration and local politicians have done differently? For once, I'd like to hear those leaders come out and say—if you threaten the life of one of our officers, he or she is going to respond in kind with force. End of story. As Wayne said, "I blame law enforcement and their handlers, and the politicians that run the police, for not saying what needs to be said." At some point, you have to stop worrying about being politically correct and speak the truth from the heart.

Then I have to ask, what were the missed opportunities we had in the Indianapolis community that would have allowed for a peaceful resolution instead of a three-year contentious community and legal battle, leaving all parties in this conflict far worse for the wear? What if, instead of protests, the Concerned Clergy encouraged community meetings to bring meaningful dialogue, processing, understanding, apologies, and forgiveness?

But it didn't happen that way.

Between our adversarial judicial system, which doesn't allow for open, vulnerable conversations between opposing sides, and a power struggle between leaders of the Concerned Clergy, that opportunity passed us by.

It does none of us any good to wish the past to change.

I asked Wayne what his thoughts were on diffusing the current tension in police/community relations. "I think you need to eliminate the extremes on both ends," he said. "You've got people like me who are heavy-handed. I believe you have to meet violence with violence, and I'll believe that until the day I die. Then you have the side who thinks it's ok to shoot at and try to kill police. You need the good and decent people who realize the truth of what's going on to stand up. They either lack the courage, or they have too much going on personally to get involved."

Wayne and I agree—the center point between the two poles is the common ground we need to get to if we're to have any chance at a resolution.

My hope is that now and in the future, we seize the opportunity we missed in 1990 before the police/community partnership deteriorates even further. For this to happen, at some point, police officers themselves need to look within. However, many of us avoid or delay that process, including myself. During one of my more recent conversations with Wayne, we discussed the way we policed back in the 80s and 90s. We were proactive. In truth, we absolutely embodied the philosophy of "the end justifies the means" in our policing. And it worked. We kept crime at bay on our watches. But it came with a price.

He told me, "Later in my career, I was in a bad place. I wrote an obituary for myself. Looking back, I realized I was not a great guy. I was a pretty violent guy." But, he admits, it came after years of experiencing the worst of humanity and having to be the one whose job it was to manage the chaos on the streets. He said, "I didn't go to work thinking I was going to mess with people because of the color of their skin. You get so overcome by the animosity, hatred, and violence directed at you on the street."

Both sides have a lot of work to do.

BACK ON THE PATH

When I was first getting sober, I met Annie Truesdell, who became a spiritual mentor of mine. I would never have met her were it not for Katy. Despite all the work I'd been doing in therapy and treatment, Katy said she felt intuitively that I hadn't reached the core of my anger and pain. One night during a dream, nearly a year after her mother passed, Katy received the message from her, "Get Scott to a medium." Knowing that though I was spiritual, I was skeptical, she went out on a limb. As a Father's Day gift, she purchased me time with a psychic medium of my choice from a local metaphysical business. Looking at their website, I reviewed all the bios of those who offered readings, and I knew intuitively who to pick. I called and set up an appointment with Annie.

Despite the website's preparatory suggestion, I arrived at my first ever reading without any questions in mind for those inhabiting the afterlife. I arrived approximately 30 minutes early and was told by the cashier that Annie was with a client but would be with me shortly. "That's ok," I responded. I arrived early on purpose so I could browse through the new-age books on their shelves, which interested me as I had just started working toward a degree in transpersonal psychology. I admit I felt a little weird being there for a reading. Transpersonal psychology or not, I was still a retired police officer and the consummate cynic. The store was not exactly a den of masculinity, but as I looked around, I saw I wasn't the only male in there, which gave me some comfort.

It was then that Annie came out of her office, walked past the two other men in the store, and said to me, "I'll be right with you, Scott."

Maybe she just got lucky, I thought to myself.

After her initial instructions on what to expect, she said, "You know Captain Snow, right?" Snow is a retiree from my department who published a book about one of his past lives.

"Yes, as a matter of fact, I do," I said.

She continued, "Perry says 'Hi'." She was referring to Perry Renn, who I mentioned in an earlier chapter. He was killed in the line of duty, sparking the "I'll Always Get Out of my Car" movement. Annie said she just had a "conversation" with Perry on the way in to work that day, and he told her someone special would be stopping by to see her. She said he had been "hanging" around her for several days now. I didn't realize it at the time I scheduled the appointment, but Annie told me the day I chose for my reading, July 5, 2017, was the anniversary of Perry's death. Exactly three years before, I was his shift captain, but was out of state in treatment when he was killed.

This took me aback. I had no time to recover when she hit me again.

"David walks with you. You know David Moore?"

The hairs on the back of my neck stood up.

I told her that I was one of David's pallbearers. Annie stood up in tears and gave me a hug. Unbeknownst to me, she told me a family member had reached out to her years ago after David's death in an attempt to reconnect with him.

Of all the psychic mediums in Indianapolis, I picked the one who talks to David Moore, my little brother.

Annie continued, "Your dad says 'Hi.' In life, he didn't believe in any of this psychic shit, but he's hopeful it will help you now."

Anyone who knew my dad knows that would have absolutely been his response.

OK, this is all beyond coincidental. Now you've got my attention, I thought.

What I began to realize, or maybe remember, after that reading is that the interconnectivity of all people is inexplicable, but the theory rings true to me. I remembered those thoughts and feelings I had before the shooting, when I began to suspect that we were all one, prompting me to read spiritual teachings and study Eastern philosophies. I remembered the sweat lodge at The Ranch with Daniel Wolfshadow, and the profound experience I had when reciting, "All my relations."   Though I didn't think it was possible, I was starting to wake up again.

I must thank Annie, who continues to hold a sort of "soul roll call" for officers killed in the line-of-duty, for the gift of liminal insight into thresholds previously unknown. It was my work with her that gave me the nudge I needed to tell this story. I now knew there was wisdom and healing to be harvested from those on the other side.

Could the notion that we're all connected help bring some understanding between the two poles in our country's police/community conflict? Collectively, my hope is that we can all move beyond the thought, "I'll believe it when I see it," to, "I'll see it when I believe it."

I had come so far. I was sober. I was in therapy. I was starting to reawaken. But I still hadn't addressed "the Beast," as my brother at The Ranch called him—the guy who could come to the surface in a rage when I felt I was being pushed or threatened. I hated that guy, yet I knew he was still there.

Soul Degree

In January 2019, six months after we completed our move to the Outer Banks, it was obvious that while our lives were better and far more stable, we were still living in survival mode. It seemed we were programmed to just get by rather than to thrive. Katy asked me to participate in an online program with her by motivational speaker Mel Robbins called Mindset Reset.

A Mindset Reset, huh? I'm definitely in need of that, I thought.

"OK, count me in," I said.

During one of the first live lectures, Mel briefly introduced her husband Chris, who mentioned a program for men called Soul Degree. It sounded like something right up my alley.

A quick search told me that Soul Degree, the brainchild of co-founder Christopher Robbins, was an adventure-inspired personal development program and retreat designed for men. It's geared specifically toward men "who aspire to stop, step back, and journey within."[195]

After reading that, Katy looked at me and said, "You have to go."

I immediately responded with my standard default—the reasons why I can't.

"I would love to," I replied, "but there's a limited number of beds, and there's an application process. There's no way I'd get selected. And besides, we really can't afford it right now." Living in paradise is a lot pricier than living in the Midwest.

"You're going," Katy said. She was employed as a barista at the very coffee shop we sat in as we researched the program. "I'll save my tips every week for the tuition if I have to, but you're going."

We drafted a short bio for my application and sent the request. The next day, I received an email from Chris Robbins himself with an incredibly kind, personal, and eloquent response that ended with, "We have a bed saved for you!"

I was excited when my itinerary arrived in the mail. It was just another one of those things in life that I knew I needed to do, but I wasn't exactly sure why when I sent my application. The preparatory guidelines asked us to start journaling on some poignant questions prior to the event: What brings you to Soul Degree? What are some of your regrets? What's a personal truth you have been ignoring? Who are you?

Where do I even start, I thought.

I drove over the sound and to the beach. There in my safe place, I started my Soul Degree journey. There, I began searching, pondering the proposed questions, and writing. As the days to departure counted down, I became increasingly anxious about one thing in particular.

According to the itinerary, the daily schedule usually ended with "campfires and cocktails."

This would be my first time away since getting sober where drinking would be an option. I discussed my anxiety with Katy in order to keep myself accountable.

The day finally came, and despite my worries, I left the Outer Banks and headed toward Vermont. On the drive there, my thoughts ran wild:

Campfires and cocktails! That sounds amazing. What happens in Vermont stays in Vermont. Wow, I can't even believe I'm entertaining that idea. I could tell them right away I don't drink. But then what would they think of me?

In early recovery, addicts learn, "First thought bad." Or like an alumnus of The Ranch once told us in a talk, "In that first year of recovery, whatever my first thought was that I wanted to do, I did exactly the opposite." That's what kept him sober.

I drove and thought, turning the ideas over and over again in my mind. I am still just one drink away from lowering my bottom even further. That I know. Unfortunately, I may always be. "Once toast, you can never go back to being just bread again." That was a statement I heard over and over in the rooms of AA, referring to those addicts who think they might be able to return to casual drinking or using one day. It may or may not be possible. Regardless, I don't ever want to play Russian roulette again by testing the waters. These days, I prefer to attend meetings of my own volition, not under court order.

I finally resolved that I would tell the guys right up front I was an alcoholic.

There in Vermont, I met some of the most amazing men I've ever known. Each of them—soul truth seekers—had an incredible story to tell, the good with the bad. That first night, as we each told our brief histories and reasons for attending, some common themes surfaced. What does it mean to be a man in today's world? Have stereotypical gender roles changed? Have I reached my own goals and expectations? Were those goals and expectations even mine to begin with? What does your path back to true self look like?

I sat there and listened intently as the others spoke. The struggles are real. More significantly, the struggles are common—struggles that men in the past were discouraged to talk about for fear of being seen as weak. Everyone seemed to have one personal truth about themselves they had been ignoring. Each of their truths, however, echoed in the next brother's testimony.

Later at campfires and cocktails, one of the guys said to me, "That's pretty cool you've been sober that long now." Then he yelled to another Soul Degree brother, "Hey, bring me another beer!" The fact that the guys heard my story and were still comfortable drinking put me at ease. Earlier, after I shared with the group, one of the attendees approached me and asked if I would prefer the group not drink. "Absolutely not," I replied. That would have not only made me miserable, but all of them as well. They didn't have a problem with alcohol, I did. I was thankful they weren't giving me the "Scott's here, hide the booze" treatment I'd grown accustomed to. They accepted me for who I was, and the cocktails weren't an issue the entire week. It was refreshing to be part of a close-knit group again.

Yoga, group exercises and discussions filled the mornings. Afternoons were spent hiking on and around the Green Mountain and part of the Appalachian Trail. One day, we were on our longest hike of the week. It was cold, raining, and blustery. As we ascended one of the brutal peaks, I couldn't help but embody that old inner friend who, as they say in the warrior world, finds pleasure in "embracing the suck." In the suck, one finds meaning and profound insight.

Somewhere along the route, we traversed through Forgiveness Leg. The thought occurred to me: at some point, you've got to forgive yourself.

As I walked out of those woods off the mountainous passage, the weather cleared immediately. I felt the warm sunlight shine on me. It felt like a brand-new day, a rebirth from three decades of intermittent, cumulative darkness and judgment of self and others. We can actually live and thrive—not just survive. I found out in order to do that, I had to let go of habitual thought patterns and limiting beliefs of self and others. As one of my Soul Degree brothers pointed out during our discussions, I had to stop judging my entire career based on the decisions I had made within a 43 second timeframe.

I also needed to let go of the ends-justifies-the-means rationalization I'd held for so long. Professionally, I became addicted to the chaos and violence associated with police work, especially when it was my immediate responsibility to intervene and dissipate it—helping those victimized by it. This is a slippery slope. Violence often begets greater violence, all in the name of defeating evil. That ideology and adherence to a warrior ethos was often in conflict with my core self. This was especially true when my desire to protect others involved force, hurting others, or taking a life in the process.

Some of these things I needed to learn along my path came into view with Soul Degree. Thank you to Chris and my other Soul Degree brothers for that gem of an experience. It's amazing what profound insight and understanding can come when those struggling with life, all for very different and unique reasons, meet on the playing field of common ground.

CHAPTER 12

FROM SACRED GROUND
TO COMMON GROUND

Here I am grounded in the present, the spring of 2022. I don't know where my professional and spiritual journey will take me from here, but I'm certain I'll know it when I get there. My goal today is to give back to the warriors and others grappling with PTSD and addiction.

This year, I completed my masters (MA) in transpersonal psychology and received my master hypnotherapist certification (MHt) at Atlantic University. I believe there is great utility in clinical and hypnotic regression work that focuses on trauma and addiction. Like Michael McGee, doctorate in hypnotherapy, stated in *Trance and Trauma: A Recovery Manual for P.T.S.D. Therapists, Veterans, and Their Families*, as hypnotherapists we can guide trauma survivors into the past to bring the darkness into light. "In the light, the shadows of the past can be defined, integrated, and healed. The return from darkness can be completed. The warrior can be fully home, both within and without."[196]

You may have heard this notion—hurt people hurt people. I like this one better—hurt people help hurt people heal.

I have also completed the Veterans Yoga Project Mindful Resilience for Trauma Training, and I am now the area manager for Eastern North Carolina. The position assists with teacher support and fund-raising efforts through direct contact with yoga teachers, studios, and businesses. Although I have a personal yoga practice, I am not a certified instructor. I am, however, working on a teacher certification in Qigong. This is another somatic modality in line with my love for the Eastern martial, and not so martial, arts. I believe that the mind is more powerful than the body. And to heal the self, one needs to evolve and connect with higher states of consciousness.

Having found a way to let go of the past and reconnect with my spiritual path again, if I die tomorrow, at least I've finally reached some peace today. But I am still a work in progress. These days, I'm learning how to effectively moderate the ego's control over my true self. It no longer serves me to get stuck in anyone's false narrative, my own included.

I think back to the therapist who warned me at the onset of this project to be careful because I might start drinking again. I heeded her warning. I remained vigilant and careful with my mental state throughout this entire process. I paused many times, sometimes for months, in an effort to process some dark memories and return to emotional homeostasis before continuing. I admit that COVID and the quarantine proved to be an unexpected challenge for me, as I know it was for many in the recovery community. But I made it to the other side of that. I think I'm a better person now that I've faced the past and put it on paper.

I am still a somewhat opinionated, steadfast warrior at heart. It's in my blood. However, warrior souls can evolve as well. When the warrior persona is not an imminent necessity and no longer serves us or those in need, we can let it go and become soul warriors.

As Steven Pressfield so eloquently said in *The Warrior Ethos,* "The Warrior Archetype is not the be-all and end-all of life. It is only one identity, one stage on the path to maturity. But it is the greatest stage—and the most powerful. It is the foundation upon which all succeeding stages are laid. Let us be, then, warriors of the heart, and enlist in our inner cause the virtues we have acquired through blood and sweat in the sphere of conflict—courage, patience, selflessness, loyalty, fidelity, self-command, respect for elders, love of our comrades (and of the enemy), perseverance, cheerfulness in adversity and a sense of humor, however terse or dark."[197]

We, the warrior collective, must find a way to meet those we protect, those we serve, and our adversaries, on the field in the center point, where collective commonalities outweigh individual narratives.

There on common ground, we can find sacred ground again— just where my journey began.

Epilogue

THE WEAPON

Reflecting back on all the opinions offered after the shooting, the absence of the gun that Barnett allegedly used during the robbery of the Taco Bell was a sticking point. I knew what I knew at the time of the shooting, and I didn't know anything else. The information I had to go on was that the suspect was armed and violent. Yet in the end, no weapon was found. If the gun had been recovered, it probably wouldn't have changed the course of what unfolded for me. It might have mattered to the protestors, but it might not have. Would that have justified my actions in their eyes? I don't know that it would have made me feel any better. If the gun had been found on the floorboard of the car, it wouldn't have changed the information I had to go on, or what actions I had already taken.

Nonetheless, I feel compelled to include the following information we received 30 years after the shooting.

During our interview with Theresa Hedge, one of the original stopping officers in the high-speed chase, she revealed to us that two years after the shooting, she was approached by a man who said he witnessed part of the chase. He was referring to what Hedge called the "Keystone Cops" scene. The man said he witnessed the driver of the Camaro spin out, stop, then roll down his window and pitch a brown paper sack with something sticking out of it. When Hedge asked him why he didn't come forward earlier, he said he didn't want to get involved because his co-workers were Black and were angry about the shooting.

Weeks after we interviewed Hedge, we spoke with Charlie Briley, the homicide detective assigned to the case. I learned for the first time that he was approached a year or more after the shooting by a man who said he witnessed the high-speed chase. According to Charlie, "The guy said specifically he had talked to a deputy up on Emerson that night, and that he gave him a phone number. He was driving a Corvette. When the Sherriff's car pulled him over and realized it wasn't who they were looking for, this guy says he thought the guy [Barnett] threw a liquor bottle or something out of the car during the chase. Says he told the Sheriff."

No Sheriff's Deputy ever came forward with that information during the time of the investigation. Charlie said they not only combed the area where Barnett was witnessed tossing something out of his car window, but he also had the Camaro turned inside out and cut apart. No weapon was ever recovered.

A Note from My Wife

When Scott first began writing this book, he expressed his apprehension over contacting the people who were in his life at the time of the shooting, including his former wife, his legal team, and his former co-workers. He didn't think they'd want any part of reliving the event, and he doubted that any of them would want to talk to him. Like many addicts do, Scott had isolated himself considerably after he retired, so reaching out to people from his past seemed an insurmountable task. Still prone to beating himself up over his alcoholism and the fall-out of it, he said to me, "I need to do this alone. I can't ask those people to help me."

As a person in recovery myself, I understood those sentiments, yet I knew intuitively that to do this story justice, he needed their input. And there was another reason I wanted to talk to those who lived it with him. As a former journalist, my instinct is to always add as much context as possible to paint the fullest picture for readers. Having been raised by two Kennedy Democrats and having lived much of my life as a bleeding-heart liberal, seeking more information is how I broaden my worldview. I adore my husband, but historically, I wouldn't have considered myself pro-police. I haven't necessarily been anti-police, either. While I knew in my heart Scott was intrinsically a good, honest person, and I believed him when he told me what happened that night at 10th and College, I still felt a need to flesh out the story with others' points of view.

I encouraged him to reconsider.

Slowly, we started putting together a list of people who might give their side of the story, as well as help Scott remember details he'd long since tucked away in his subconscious. The responses we received from those we contacted move me to tears even now as I think of them.

We started with an easy one—Fitz. Still one of his best friends, Scott knew Fitz would at least entertain his questions. His response was, "Absolutely. Anything you need. Call me any time." The countless phone interviews that followed with Fitz were invaluable.

That gave Scott the courage he needed to continue.

We reached out to Wayne Voida, the first person to talk to Scott after the shooting. Just like Fitz, Wayne took our calls and talked to us for hours several times throughout the process. I'll never forget during one interview when Wayne said to us, "That was my first police shooting. I was not OK, but in another way, I was OK, because it was Scott." It was clear that in 1990, as well as today, Wayne holds a great amount of respect and affection for his old friend and former SWAT teammate.

With some trepidation, we reached out to Tammy, his former wife. "Anything you need," she said to us, "I'm happy to help." Of all the people we contacted, her response moved me the most. With no hesitation and holding nothing back, Tammy generously gave us her time and attention and walked us through the past from her point of view. What an invaluable contribution, and what a testament to both Tammy and Scott's character.

We reached out to Theresa Hedge, one of the first responding officers when the Barnett robbery was reported. She sent us her number and told us to call her any time. Later when I thanked her, she said, "You're welcome. He was my academy classmate. He was our top guy! I've always had great respect for him."

Then there was Jeff Avington, a Black police officer who worked with Scott, and one of the first to arrive on the scene that night. He expressed his disappointment at how Scott was being portrayed in the media and within the Black community after the incident. He said, "If they wanted to get a true opinion of Scott, they could have gone over to where he worked, around Winthrop, in the hood. They knew him, and they liked him. They were more willing to talk to Scott than they were to any other officer. He knew the bad guys, and they respected him a lot. It didn't matter who was Black or white. It was just good guy or bad guy." Jeff also told us he was just a few blocks away from the intersection when Barnett crashed the Camaro. "It could just as easily have been me instead of Scott," he said.

The responses were all the same. From his former wife to his former co-workers, it was clear to me that all of these people still had great love for Scott. I've only had the pleasure of knowing him since 2015, and though I suspected as much, it was heart-warming to witness the amazing man I knew and loved through the eyes of his past associates. It was an honor to walk this journey with him, helping him find the right words, and giving him encouragement to keep going when he faltered. My strength through this process came from the people on that list who selflessly gave us their time and shared their minds and hearts with us. I am forever grateful to them for helping us write this story.

Postscript: I also tried to contact Brad Wisely, Leonard Barnett's roommate at the time of the incident. I wanted Leonard's side to be told by a person who he seemed to be close to at that time. I attempted to reach Brad via email and snail mail, but he did not reply. In an effort to respect his privacy and choice, I did not pursue it further.

A NOTE TO MY FATHER

Hey Dad, turns out I grew up to be just like you. Except, of course, for all the balanced and grounded facets I got from Mom. And I couldn't be prouder of that. That includes the love and light, the dark shadow we possess, and our life-long quest to find equanimity between the two poles. I still have the handwritten letter you sent me in the weeks immediately after the shooting. It was prophetic then, still true today, and brings tears to my eyes whenever I read it. It's also great advice for any police officer who might be questioning the actions he or she took in the line of duty.

Scott...

After talking with you at the range this morning, I know you are upset with all the bullshit. But you and I and one hell of a lot of other people know you did the right thing... You must remember, there will always be the group of people who want to start shit, but believe me they are the minority and not the majority... You keep that head screwed on right! Forget the shit-slingers and think about the good people you protect every time you go out there!! The shit-slingers can say what they want but only you can control your mind and its thoughts so keep it right. Your Mom and I support and love you and we respect you as a man. Hang tough.

Love Dad

I tried my best. Love you too, Dad. I'll see you on the other side.

Acknowledgments

Thank you...

To my beautiful wife and beloved soul mate Katy: If it were not for your unconditional love, enduring support through this writing endeavor, and gift of the golden pen, my life and manuscript would still be an utter train wreck.

To Mom: for her unconditional love and support through some of my darkest hours. She gave birth to me and birth to my second chance at life decades later through addiction rehab support. I took your advice, Mom. I wrote a book.

To Madi and Matthew: I try every day to be a better father to make up for lost time.

To John Kautzman, attorney at Law: We were both young and embarking on our chosen careers. Through your legal prowess, passion, and defense, you opened the door to the remaining two-thirds of my life. You, my friend, defend the Thin Blue Line by defending those who defend the Thin Blue Line. I am forever grateful.

To Danny Overley: Were it not for your unwavering support, I may not have found the strength to move forward during some of the darkest hours of my personal and professional life. As founding chairman of the Indiana FOP Critical Incident/Memorial Team, you have helped far too many families of police officers bury their loved one.

To Tammy Snyder Haslar: At such a request as mine, many women would have told their cheating ex-husband to go fuck off. You didn't. Thank you for sharing your part of this story. And lest I forget btw, thank you for saving my life, literally!

To my sister-in-law Nancy Pieters Mayfield: If it were not for your editing genius and devoting so much of your own personal time, the Book Baby editing team would have had a great deal of work ahead of them before publishing.

To Jonathan Thompson: my vagabond friend and fellow Soul Degree brother whose creativity and photography you see on the front and back covers of this book. I intend to see your work on many more books and the big screen someday soon.

To all those friends who graciously gave of their time to be interviewed: Theresa Hedge, Wayne Voida, Jeff Avington, Stephen "Fitz" Fitzpatrick, Jo Moore, Tom Black, Charlie Briley, Chris Robbins, James Gray, Charlie Frangos, Danny Overley

To all the people I named between the covers of this book who have shared my journey with me. Some I liked and some I didn't. Either way, they shaped me into the person I have become and helped me fulfill my eternal soul contract.

And finally, to the writers and cast of *Sons of Anarchy*: If it weren't for binging your last season with a few cocktails on board, I may never have known what it was like to be the handcuffed, and not just the one doing the handcuffing. That is eye-opening!

SOLITUDE'S LAST DANCE

Daunting voices from the dark
The fathomless depths,
Alone, I park.
Visions of 'I' and 'me', I have of self,
Sit high upon a black veiled shelf.

A collusive being of unconscious morbidity
Purported feelings of self-worth,
An inexplicable lucidity.
The hopes, dreams, and beauty of things, so distant and far.
Like touching the horizon or a falling star.

The eternal beauty of nature's collage',
From the flowers of Spring to Fall's decay,
An ephemeral mirage.
The sun rises and sets yet never apart.
The twisted notion of fate, a perfected art.

The process of individuation,
Embracing the rhizome
Through introspective creation.

Procreates illusory apparitions of persona, shadows, and soul,
An inescapable quagmire's intrinsically infinite black hole.

Helping hands abound and near,
Germinate fear of revelation, by
Those unconditionally dear.
Again, cast by thine-self to wolves unknown,
The remaining monolith, still all alone.

Placid waters at dusk's descent,
Distorted reflections of a decaying soul's
Immanent personal atonement.
Fondest memories, long since past,
Myopia's nonexistent future, present at last.

Darkness approaches, midnight's cloaked chance,
The paradoxical fortuitous of
Solitude's Last Dance.
With insurmountable mountains to climb,
Time shortened of morbid volition, a bittersweet rhyme.

Sailing against gale force winds, a laborious chore,
A desperate, cold, and lonely adherence to
One's life anchors.
Light the eyes of chance through tempestuous furry break,
A golden beacon of hope whose passage might make.

Scott L. Haslar
c. mid-1990s

Endnotes

1   McManus, E. R. (2019). *The way of the warrior: An ancient path to inner peace.* Waterbrook. p. 1.

2   Truesdell, A. (2010). *A butterfly in the garden.* Godsign Institute. P. 53.

3   Retrieved from. https//www.indianaBlackexpo.com/about-history.asp

4   *Jet* Magazine. (1990, Sept. 10, Vol. 78, No. 22). "Giving makes IBE's 20ᵗʰ birthday a special success": A Johnson Publication. P. 25.

5   *Indianapolis Recorder.* Retrieved from: http/nwtimes.com/ uncategorized/Indiana-Black-expo-celebrates-years-of-honoring/ article.

6   Staff Reporter. (1990, July 21). Expo explodes with excitement. *The Indianapolis Recorder,* p. A1.

7   Gadzekpo, A. (1990, July 7) Expo's entertainment hotter than ever. *The Indianapolis Recorder.* p. B1.

8   Trusnik, M. (1990, July 9). Police shoot man after car crash. *The Indianapolis News.* PP. A1-A2.

9   Patterson, J. (1990, July 10). Robbery suspect killed by police. *The Indianapolis Star.* Pp. 1-2.

10 Hooper, K. (1990, July 14). Another Black slain by IPD? *The Indianapolis Recorder.* P. A15.

11 Morgan, K. (1990, July 12). Police shooting spurs call for probe. *The Indianapolis Star.* P. 13.

12 Patterson, J. (1990, July 10). Robbery suspect killed by police. *The Indianapolis Star.* P2.

13 Hooper, K. (1990, July 14). Another Black slain by IPD? *The Indianapolis Recorder.* PP A1, A15.

14 Patterson, J. (1990, July 11). Watchdog group criticizes police shooting: Officer's use of 9mm gun questioned. *The Indianapolis Star.* P. D1.

15 Hooper, K. (1990, July 14). Another Black slain by IPD? *The Indianapolis Recorder.* P. 1.

16   Morgan, K. (1990, July 29). Police chief Annee defends department's shooting record. *The Indianapolis Star.* P1.

17   Morgan, K. (1990, July 12). Police shooting spurs call for probe. *The Indianapolis Star.* P. 13.

18   Shull, R. (1990, July 13). Shooting death a beginning, not an end. *The Indianapolis News.* P. A-3.

19   Shull, R. (1990, July 13). Shooting death a beginning, not an end. *The Indianapolis News.* P. A-3.

20   Stokes, D. (1990, July 14). FBI to probe police shooting. *The Indianapolis News.* P. B-1.

21   Morgan, K. (1990, July 12). Police shooting spurs call for probe. *The Indianapolis Star.* P. 1.

22   Lacy, B. (1990, July 29). Dirty Harry of Indianapolis not afraid to fire. *The Indianapolis Star.* P. 1.

23   Lacy, B. (1990, July 29). Dirty Harry of Indianapolis not afraid to fire. *The Indianapolis Star.* P. C8.

24   Lacy, B. (1990, July 17). Jackson calls for outrage over racial violence. *The Indianapolis Star.* P. 1.

25   Lacy, B. (1990, July 17). Jackson calls for outrage over racial violence. *The Indianapolis Star.* pp. 1, 10.

26   Lacy, B. (1990, July 17). Jackson calls for outrage over racial violence. *The Indianapolis Star.* pp. 1, 10.

27   Lacy, B. (1990, July 17). Jackson calls for outrage over racial violence. *The Indianapolis Star.* pp. 1, 10.

28   Lacy, B. (1990, July 17). Jackson calls for outrage over racial violence. *The Indianapolis Star.* pp. 1, 10.

29   Morgan, K. (1990, July 14). Annee backs policeman in shooting; FBI investigating. *The Indianapolis Star.* pp. 1, 6.

30   Ford, L. (1990, July 16). Hudnut pleads for easing of racial tension. *The Indianapolis Star.* pp. 1, 5.

31   Ford, L. (1990, July 16). Hudnut pleads for easing of racial tension. *The Indianapolis Star.* pp. 1, 5.

32   Ford, L. (1990, July 16). Hudnut pleads for easing of racial tension. *The Indianapolis Star.* pp. 1, 5.

33   Ford, L. (1990, July 16). Hudnut pleads for easing of racial tension. *The Indianapolis Star.* pp. 1, 5.

34   Ford, L. (1990, July 16). Hudnut pleads for easing of racial tension. *The Indianapolis Star.* pp. 1, 5.

35   Heckman, F. (1990, July 17, July 18). Commentary. Indianapolis, IN: WIBC 1070.

36 Alexander, W. (July 1990). Shooting of unarmed man seems unjustified. *The Indianapolis Recorder.*

37 Patterson, J. (1990, July 18). Mother of slain man files police complaint. *The Indianapolis Star.* p. D1.

38 I.M.P.D General Order 1.31, retrieved April 2019 from www. indyogve.org.

39 Patterson, J., Lacy, B. (1990, July 24). Shooting of robbery suspect was justified, firearms board rules. *The Indianapolis Star.* P.1.

40 Patterson, J., Lacy, B. (1990, July 24). Shooting of robbery suspect was justified, firearms board rules. *The Indianapolis Star.* P.10.

41 Zogg, J. (1990, July 31) Ministers, backers seek funding to probe police-action shooting. *The Indianapolis News.* Pp A1, A8.

42 Patterson, J. (1990, July 31). 30 ministers lead protest of shooting. *The Indianapolis Star.* P1, P6.

43 Patterson, J. (1990, July 31). 30 ministers lead protest of shooting. *The Indianapolis Star.* P1, P6.

44 Zogg, J. (1990, July 31). Shooting: 200 at protest. *The Indianapolis News.* P. A8.

45 Patterson, J. (1990, July 31). 30 ministers lead protest of shooting. *The Indianapolis Star.* P1, P6.

46 Patterson, J. (1990, July 31). 30 ministers lead protest of shooting. *The Indianapolis Star.* P1, P6.

47 Lacy, B., Patterson, J. (1990, July 24). Shooting of robbery suspect was justified, firearms board rules. *The Indianapolis Star.* p. 1, 10.

48 Harris, W. (1990, August 1). Raises questions on shooting. *The Indianapolis News.* p. A15.

49 Ford, L. (1990, August 3). Coroner backs police action following chase. *The Indianapolis Star.* Pp. 1, 15.

50 Ford, L. (1990, August 3). Coroner backs police action following chase. *The Indianapolis Star.* Pp. 1, 15.

51 Ford, L. (1990, August 3). Coroner backs police action following chase. *The Indianapolis Star.* Pp. 1, 15.

52 Traub, P. (1990, Aug. 5). City needs credible review process for police shootings. *The Indianapolis Star.* P. F-7.

53 Traub, P. (1990, Aug. 5). City needs credible review process for police shootings. *The Indianapolis Star.* P. F-7.

54 Remondini, D. (1990, August 7). Ministers' rally calls for boycott, resignations. *The Indianapolis Star.* Pp. 1, 10.

55 Morgan, K. (1990, August, 5). Goldsmith to speed probe of robbery suspect's death. *The Indianapolis Star.* P. 1 P. 8.

56 Morgan, K. (1990, August 12). Friends, family, city—all new a
different Barnett. *The Indianapolis Star.* P1, P.10.

57 Zogg, J. (1990, July 25). Dead man linked to purse grab. *The
Indianapolis News.* P. B1.

58 Morgan, K. (1990, August 12). Friends, family, city—all new a
different Barnett. *The Indianapolis Star.* P1, P.10.

59 Morgan, K. (1990, August 12). Friends, family, city—all new a
different Barnett. *The Indianapolis Star.* P1, P.10.

60 Morgan, K. (1990, August 12). Friends, family, city—all new a
different Barnett. *The Indianapolis Star.* P1, P.10.

61 Morgan, K. (1990, August 12). Friends, family, city—all new a
different Barnett. *The Indianapolis Star.* P1, P.10.

62 Morgan, K. (1990, August 12). Friends, family, city—all new a
different Barnett. *The Indianapolis Star.* P1, P.10.

63 Morgan, K. (1990, August 12). Friends, family, city—all new a
different Barnett. *The Indianapolis Star.* P1, P.10.

64 Morgan, K. (1990, August 12). Friends, family, city—all new a
different Barnett. *The Indianapolis Star.* P1, P.10.

65 Morgan, K. (1990, August 12). Friends, family, city—all new a
different Barnett. *The Indianapolis Star.* P1, P.10.

66 Morgan, K. (1990, August 12). Friends, family, city—all new a
different Barnett. *The Indianapolis Star.* P1, P.10.

67 Petroskey, D. (1990, August 13). Fatal shooting by police puts mayor,
minister at odds again. *The Indianapolis Star.* p. 1.

68 Zogg, J. (1990, August 16). Hearing on another Haslar issue studied.
The Indianapolis News. P. D1.

69 Morgan, K. (1990 October 4). Teen who accused patrolman of
brutality is held in slaying. *The Indianapolis Star.* p. D1.

70 Morgan, K. (1990 August 15). Mayor promises Black pastors more
talks on police policies. *The Indianapolis Star.* P.1.

71 Morgan, K. (1990 August 15). Mayor promises Black pastors more
talks on police policies. *The Indianapolis Star.* P.16.

72 Morgan, K. (1990 August 15). Mayor promises Black pastors more
talks on police policies. *The Indianapolis Star.* P.16.

73 Petroskey, D. (1990, August 16). Mayor torn by number of clergy
seeking audience. *The Indianapolis Star.* pp. B1, B8.

74 Morgan, K. (1990 October 5). City plans closer look at police
shootings. *The Indianapolis Star.* Pp. 1, 11.

75 Gillaspy, J., Patterson, J. (1990 October 16). U.S. clears policeman in
Barnett case. *The Indianapolis Star.* P. 1, P. 10.

76 Gillaspy, J., Patterson, J. (1990 October 16). U.S. clears policeman in Barnett case. *The Indianapolis Star.* P. 1, P. 10.

77 Gillaspy, J., Patterson, J. (1990 October 16). U.S. clears policeman in Barnett case. *The Indianapolis Star.* P. 1, P. 10.

78 Gillaspy, J. (1990 October 18) Barnett's parents sue police officer. *The Indianapolis Star.* Pp 1, 4.

79 Gillaspy, J., Patterson, J. (1990 October 16). U.S. clears policeman in Barnett case. *The Indianapolis Star.* P. 1, P. 10

80 Albert, B. (1990 December 12). Policeman cleared in fatal shooting. *The Indianapolis Star.* P. 1, 12.

81 Albert, B. (1990 December 12). Policeman cleared in fatal shooting. *The Indianapolis Star.* P. 1, 12.

82 Morgan, K. (1991 March 8). Controversial cop gets medal: Lauded for actions in Barnett shooting. *The Indianapolis Star.* Pp. 1, 4.

83 Morgan, K. (1991 March 8). Controversial cop gets medal: Lauded for actions in Barnett shooting. *The Indianapolis Star.* Pp. 1, 4.

84 Morgan, K. (1991 March 8). Controversial cop gets medal: Lauded for actions in Barnett shooting. *The Indianapolis Star.* P. 1, P. 4.p

85 Morgan, K. (1991 March 8). Controversial cop gets medal: Lauded for actions in Barnett shooting. *The Indianapolis Star.* Pp. 1, 4.

86 Petroskey, D. (1991, March 14). Police chief should be fired, Democratic candidate says. *The Indianapolis Star.* P. C7.

87 Patterson, J. (1991, March 13). Police medal brings cries of outrage. *The Indianapolis Star.* pp. 1, 13.

88 Patterson, J. (1991, March 13). Police medal brings cries of outrage. *The Indianapolis Star.* pp. 1, 13.

89 Patterson, J. (1991, March 13). Police medal brings cries of outrage. *The Indianapolis Star.* pp. 1, 13.

90 Patterson, J. (1991 March 19). Rescind or resign: Group targets Annee, medal of valor. *The Indianapolis Star.* p.B1

91 Patterson, J. (1991 March 19). Rescind or resign: Group targets Annee, medal of valor. *The Indianapolis Star.* p.B1

92 Patterson, J. (1991 March 19). Rescind or resign: Group targets Annee, medal of valor. *The Indianapolis Star.* p.B1

93 Morgan, K. (1991 March 21). Controversy over police award prompts apology from chief. *The Indianapolis Star.* P. 1.

94 Morgan, K. (1991 March 21). Controversy over police award prompts apology from chief. *The Indianapolis Star.* Pp. 1, 16.

95 Petroskey, D. (1991 March 22). Haslar deserved award, panelists say. *The Indianapolis Star.* Pp. 1, 9.

96 Petroskey, D. (1991 March 22). Haslar deserved award, panelists say. *The Indianapolis Star.* Pp. 1, 9.

97 Cunningham, G. (1991 March 21). The message of the Haslar medal. *The Indianapolis Star.* p A9.

98 Cunningham, G. (1991 March 21). The message of the Haslar medal. *The Indianapolis Star.* p A9.

99 Whitehead, H. (1991 March 21). Excessive force. *The Indianapolis Star. Letters* p. A9.

100 Davidson, H. (1991 March 21). An award for a shooting. *The Indianapolis Star.* P. A9.

101 Schreiber, B. (1991 March 21). Racial motives. *The Indianapolis Star.* P. A9.

102 Newborn, E. (1991 March 31). The duty of police. *The Indianapolis Star.* P. F3.

103 Hutchinson, E. (1991 April 4). The Concerned Clergy and crime. *The Indianapolis Star.* p. A15.

104 Morgan, K. (1991 July 7). A year after the shooting…Barnett's death changed attitudes of those caught in controversy. *The Indianapolis Star.* P. F1, F5.

105 Morgan, K. (1991 July 7). A year after the shooting…Barnett's death changed attitudes of those caught in controversy. *The Indianapolis Star.* P. F1, F5.

106 Morgan, K. (1991 July 7). A year after the shooting…Barnett's death changed attitudes of those caught in controversy. *The Indianapolis Star.* P. F1, F5.

107 Morgan, K. (1991 July 7). A year after the shooting…Barnett's death changed attitudes of those caught in controversy. *The Indianapolis Star.* P. F1, F5.

108 Morgan, K. (1991 July 7). A year after the shooting…Barnett's death changed attitudes of those caught in controversy. *The Indianapolis Star.* P. F1, F5.

109 Morgan, K. (1991 July 7). A year after the shooting…Barnett's death changed attitudes of those caught in controversy. *The Indianapolis Star.* P. F1, F5.

110 Morgan, K. (1991 July 7). A year after the shooting…Barnett's death changed attitudes of those caught in controversy. *The Indianapolis Star.* P. F1, F5.

111 Morgan, K. (1991 July 7). A year after the shooting…Barnett's death changed attitudes of those caught in controversy. *The Indianapolis Star.* P. F1, F5.

112 O'Neal, K. (1992, Sept 12). Jury selection to begin in police shooting case. *The Indianapolis News.* Pp. A1, A8.

113 O'Neal, K. (1992, Sept 12). Jury selection to begin in police shooting case. *The Indianapolis News*. Pp. A1, A8.

114 Patterson, J. (1992). Trial to begin for IPD officer sued in slaying. *The Indianapolis Star*. P. C1.

115 O'Neill, J. (1992 September 15). Barnett didn't go for a gun, lawyer says. *The Indianapolis Star*. P. B1-2.

116 O'Neill, J. (1992 September 15). Barnett didn't go for a gun, lawyer says. *The Indianapolis Star*. P. B1-2.

117 O'Neal, K. (1992, Sept 15). Witness disputes officer's account. *The Indianapolis News*. P. 8.

118 O'Neal, K. (1992, Sept 15). Witness disputes officer's account. *The Indianapolis News*. P. 8.

119 O'Neill, J. (1992 September 15). Barnett didn't go for a gun, lawyer says. *The Indianapolis Star*. P. B1-2.

120 O'Neal, K. (1992, Sept 15). Witness disputes officer's account. *The Indianapolis News*. P. 8.

121 O'Neal, K. (1992, Sept 15). Witness disputes officer's account. *The Indianapolis News*. P. 8.

122 O'Neill, J. (1992 September 15). Barnett not going for a gun, lawyer says. *The Indianapolis Star*. P. B1-2.

123 O'Neal, K. (1992, Sept, 15). Witness saw no attack on police. *The Indianapolis News*. P. C1, C2.

124 O'Neal, K. (1992, Sept, 15). Witness saw no attack on police. *The Indianapolis News*. P. C1, C2.

125 O'Neal, K. (1992, Sept. 16). Police videotape shows money bags inside car. *The Indianapolis News*. P. B1, B2.

126 Patterson, J. (1992, September, 16). Orthopedist says suspect couldn't walk. *The Indianapolis Star*. Pp. B1-2.

127 Patterson, J. (1992, September, 16). Orthopedist says suspect couldn't walk. *The Indianapolis Star*. Pp. B1-2.

128 Patterson, J. (1992, September, 16). Orthopedist says suspect couldn't walk. *The Indianapolis Star*. Pp. B1-2.

129 O'Neal, K. (1992, Sept 17). Blue line supports patrolman: But Black spectator doubts officer's testimony on fatal shooting. *The Indianapolis News*. Pp. C1, C2.

130 O'Neal, K. (1992, Sept 17). Blue line supports patrolman: But Black spectator doubts officer's testimony on fatal shooting. *The Indianapolis News*. Pp. C1, C2.

131 O'Neal, K. (1992, Sept 17). Blue line supports patrolman: But Black spectator doubts officer's testimony on fatal shooting. *The Indianapolis News*. Pp. C1, C2.

132 Patterson, J. (1992, Sept 17). Officer says he fended off Barnett. *The Indianapolis Star.* p. C-1.

133 O'Neal, K. (1992, Sept 17). Blue line supports patrolman: But Black spectator doubts officer's testimony on fatal shooting. *The Indianapolis News.* Pp. C1, C2.

134 Patterson, J. (1992, Sept 17). Officer says he fended off Barnett. *The Indianapolis Star.* p. C-1.

135 Patterson, J. (1992, Sept 17). Officer says he fended off Barnett. *The Indianapolis Star.* p. C-1.

136 O'Neal, K. (1992, Sept 17). Blue line supports patrolman: But Black spectator doubts officer's testimony on fatal shooting. *The Indianapolis News.* Pp. C1, C2.

137 O'Neal, K. (1992, Sept 17). Blue line supports patrolman: But Black spectator doubts officer's testimony on fatal shooting. *The Indianapolis News.* Pp. C1, C2.

138 Patterson, J. (1992 September 18) Barnett could walk, doctor testifies. *The Indianapolis Star.* P. C1-C2.

139 Patterson, J. (1992 September 18) Barnett could walk, doctor testifies. *The Indianapolis Star.* P. C1-C2.

140 Patterson, J. (1992 September 18) Barnett could walk, doctor testifies. *The Indianapolis Star.* P. C1-C2.

141 Patterson, J. (1992 September 18) Barnett could walk, doctor testifies. *The Indianapolis Star.* P. C1-C2.

142 Patterson, J. (1992 September 19). Jury deliberating civil rights case. *The Indianapolis Star.* P. B1-2.

143 Patterson, J. (1992 September 19). Jury deliberating civil rights case. *The Indianapolis Star.* P. B1-2.

144 Patterson, J. (1992 September 19). Jury deliberating civil rights case. *The Indianapolis Star.* P. B1-2.

145 Patterson, J. (1992 September 19). Jury deliberating civil rights case. *The Indianapolis Star.* P. B1-2.

146 Patterson, J. (1992 September 20). Jury deadlocks; officer will face another trial. *The Indianapolis Star.* P. 1-2.

147 Patterson, J. (1992 September 20). Jury deadlocks; officer will face another trial. *The Indianapolis Star.* P. 1-2.

148 Patterson, J. (1992 September 20). Jury deadlocks; officer will face another trial. *The Indianapolis Star.* P. 1-2.

149 Gillaspy, J. (1993 January 30). Pastor blasts promotion of Haslar to sergeant. *The Indianapolis Star.* P. B1-2.

150 Gillaspy, J. (1993 January 30). Pastor blasts promotion of Haslar to sergeant. *The Indianapolis Star.* P. B1-2.

151 Gillaspy, J. (1993 January 30). Pastor blasts promotion of Haslar to sergeant. *The Indianapolis Star.* P. B1-2.

152 Horne, T. (1993 January 30). Officer's promotion draws fire: New sergeant faces suit in fatal 1990 shooting. *The Indianapolis News.*

153 Horne, T. (1993 January 30). Officer's promotion draws fire: New sergeant faces suit in fatal 1990 shooting. *The Indianapolis News.*

154 Gillaspy, J. (1993 January 30). Pastor blasts promotion of Haslar to sergeant. *The Indianapolis Star.* P. B1-2.

155 Voida, W. (1993, Feb. 14). Defending a police officer's promotion. *The Indianapolis Star. p. F-3.*

156 O'Neal, K. (1993 February 9). Defense hints at HIV testimony in Haslar's trial. *The Indianapolis News.* P. D1-2.

157 Patterson, J. (1993 February 8) 2nd trial in shooting starts today. *The Indianapolis Star.* P. 1-2.

158 O'Neal, K. (1993 February 8). Jurors may hear testimony on HIV. *The Indianapolis News.* P. D1-2.

159 O'Neal, K. (1993 February 8). Jurors may hear testimony on HIV. *The Indianapolis News.* P. D1-2.

160 O'Neill, J. (1993 February 9). Retrial opens in civil rights suit against officer. *The Indianapolis Star.* p. A12.

161 O'Neal, K. (1993 February 9). Defense hints at HIV testimony in Haslar's trial. *The Indianapolis News.* P. D1-2.

162 O'Neal, K. (1993 February 9). Defense hints at HIV testimony in Haslar's trial. *The Indianapolis News.* P. D1-2.

163 O'Neill, J. (1993 February 9). Retrial opens in civil rights suit against officer. *The Indianapolis Star.* p. A12.

164 O'Neal, K. (1993 February 8). Jurors may hear testimony on HIV. *The Indianapolis News.* P. D1-2.

165 O'Neill, J. (1993 February 9). Retrial opens in civil rights suit against officer. *The Indianapolis Star.* p. A12.

166 O'Neill, J. (1993 February 9). Retrial opens in civil rights suit against officer. *The Indianapolis Star.* p. A12.

167 O'Neill, J. (1993 February 12). Jurors hear radio call from shooting of suspect. *Indianapolis Star.* p. D4.

168 O'Neal, K. (1993, February 11). Barnett had AIDS virus, says doctor. *The Indianapolis News.* P. D1.

169 O'Neal, K. (1993 February 10) Witnesses dispute earning potential. *The Indianapolis News.* P. E1.

170 O'Neill, J. (1993 February 10) Barnett could not walk, jurors told. *The Indianapolis Star.* P. 1-2.

171 O'Neal, K. (1993 February 10) Witnesses dispute earning potential. *The Indianapolis News*. P. E1.

172 O'Neill, J. (1993 February 13). Policeman vindicated in shooting case. *The Indianapolis Star*. P.1-2).

173 O'Neill, J. (1993 February 13). Policeman vindicated in shooting case. *The Indianapolis Star*. P.1-2).

174 O'Neill, J. (1993 February 13). Policeman vindicated in shooting case. *The Indianapolis Star*. P.1-2).

175 Patterson, J. (1993 February 14). Trooper's death swayed jurors in Haslar trial, attorneys agree. *The Indianapolis Star*. P. 1-2.

176 Patterson, J. (1993 February 14). Trooper's death swayed jurors in Haslar trial, attorneys agree. *The Indianapolis Star*. P. 1-2.

177 Patterson, J. (1993 February 14). Trooper's death swayed jurors in Haslar trial, attorneys agree. *The Indianapolis Star*. P. 1-2.

178 Bibbs, R., Fleming, M. (1993, Feb 13). Police, Blacks see ruling in different light. *The Indianapolis News*. Pp. A1, A2.

179 Moore, B. (1998, Jan 21). Business as usual in latest police probe. *The Indianapolis Star*. p. A-11.

180 Murray, J. (2010, August 27). New leader named for East District. *The Indianapolis Star*. P. B1, B4.

181 Murray, J. (2010, August 27). New leader named for East District. *The Indianapolis Star*. P. B1, B4.

182 Galer, S. (2010, Aug 26). Retrieved from http://wthr.com/article/new-east-district-commander-addresses-1990-shooting

183 Galer, S. (2010, Aug 26). Retrieved from http://wthr.com/article/new-east-district-commander-addresses-1990-shooting

184 Galer, S. (2010, Aug 26). Retrieved from http://wthr.com/article/new-east-district-commander-addresses-1990-shooting

185 Ajabu, M. (2013). Retrieved from: http://ajabuspeaks.squarespace.com/ajabu-speaks/2013/2/21/international-action-against-police-brutality.html

186 Ajabu, M. (2013). Retrieved from: http://ajabuspeaks.squarespace.com/ajabu-speaks/2013/2/21/international-action-against-police-brutality.html

187 Rehagen, T. (2008, December). In the name of the father. *Indianapolis Monthly*. Retreived from http://indianapolismonthly.com/longform/im-crime-files-in-the-name-of-the-father-mmoja-ajabu

188 Ajabu, M. (2013). Retrieved from: http://ajabuspeaks.squarespace.com/ajabu-speaks/2013/2/21/international-action-against-police-brutality.html

189 Penner, D. (2011, Jan 24). Answers sought in cop's shooting. *The Indianapolis Star*. pp. A1, A4.

190 Penner, D. (2011, Jan 24). Answers sought in cop's shooting. *The Indianapolis Star*. pp. A1, A4.

191 Penner, D. (2011, Jan 24). Answers sought in cop's shooting. *The Indianapolis Star*. pp. A1, A4.

192 Tuohy, J. (2013, July 18). IMPD targeting crime hot spots. *The Indianapolis Star*. p. A1, A6.

193 Hunter, C.R., Eimer, B. (2017). *The art of hypnotic regression therapy: A clinical guide*. Crown House Publishing. P. 164.

194 Guerra, K. (2014, July 7). The city was attacked. *The Indianapolis Star*. p. A1, A8.

195 Robbins, C. (2019). Retrieved from www.souldegree.com.

196 McGee, M. (2010). Trance and trauma: A recovery manual for PTSD therapists, veterans, and their families. Transpersonal Publishing. P. xiv.

197 Pressfield, S. (2011). *The warrior ethos*. Black Irish Entertainment.